QUANTUM LEAP

Quantum Leap

Tools for Managing Companies in the New Economy

Jacques Chaize

www.jacques-chaize.com

Translated by Michael Cain

First published 2000 by
PALGRAVE
Houndmills, Basingstoke, Hampshire RG21 6XS and
175 Fifth Avenue, New York, N.Y. 10010
Companies and representatives throughout the world

PALGRAVE is the new global academic imprint of
St. Martin's Press LLC Scholarly and Reference Division and
Palgrave Publishers Ltd (formerly Macmillan Press Ltd).

ISBN 0–333–92898–9

This book is printed on paper suitable for recycling and
made from fully managed and sustained forest sources.

A catalogue record for this book is available
from the British Library.

Library of Congress Cataloging-in-Publication Data

Chaize, Jacques.
  [Grand écart. English].
  The quantum leap : tools for managing companies in the new
economy / Jacques Chaize ; translated by Michael Cain.
      p. cm.
  Includes bibliographical references and index.
  ISBN 0–333–92898–9
    1. Organizational change. 2. Business enterprises—
Technological innovations. 3. Globalization. 4. Corporate
culture. I. Title: Tools for managing companies in the new
economy. II. Title.

HD58.8 .C42413 2000

                                                    00–059133

Editing and origination by
Aardvark Editorial, Mendham, Suffolk

10 9 8 7 6 5 4 3 2 1
09 08 07 06 05 04 03 02 01 00

Printed and bound in Great Britain by
Creative Print & Design (Wales), Ebbw Vale

To José Guillermo Urrutia Nieto

Contents

Acknowledgements

This book is the fruit of experience, research, dialogues and shared learning. In the first place, I would like to thank all the members of the 'Progrès des Entreprises' Commission, and particularly Emmanuel d'André, Pierre Bellon, Natalie de Chalus, Bernard Ducass, Jean-Marie Descarpentries, Brigitte de Gastines, Jacques Giroire, Jean-Marie Laborde, Pierre-Antoine Gailly, Alain Fribourg and Jacques Lefèvre, as well as all those who have passed on to me any number of the ideas, words and images reproduced here.

My thanks are also extended to Amaury de Warenghien, Jacques Lebraty and Catherine Thomas, whose work and writings concerning the hierarchy and the piloting of change have been a decisive influence; to Yves Rajaud, Claude Levy-Leboyer and Alain Gauthier, who have passed on to me invaluable ideas concerning motivation and dialogue; to Manfred Mack, Max Boisot, Laurent Cousin, Françoise Litou and Vibeke Gustafsson for their theoretical knowledge and concrete experience of learning.

Special thanks are also due to all those within my company and the Danfoss group who are building up together, day by day, the hypertext company, in particular Ole Steen Andersen, Gunnar Daehlin, Frédéric Fiancette, Joseph Sassonia and Jean Tolon.

Finally, I owe a debt of gratitude to Marie, Laetitia, Diane and Emeric for their constant patience.

Introduction

Our task is to order our manners rather than order our letters.

Montaigne

Beijing, May 2018. Hardly three hours after leaving Paris, the supersonic jumbo jet lands noiselessly on the tarmac shining in the evening rain. In the distance, hemmed in by the flaming red towers that now encircle the airport, the golden arch of a temple reaches up to a leaden sky. Twenty years ago, it dominated the whole horizon.

That was in the spring of 1998. We had arranged to meet in China for a strategic seminar. At that time I was using a state-of-the-art laptop computer, weighing less than two kilos, connected to the Internet, the ancestor of the present NGI.[1] Coming from New York, Singapore and Chalon-sur-Saône, we had prepared our proposals in advance by electronic mail. Wishing to travel light, I had decided not to print out texts and overheads until my arrival. At the airport I met one of the other delegates. He was bent double under the weight of his suitcases, mostly full of documents printed out by his secretary before his departure. He passed an ironic remark on the lightness of my luggage, but my explanation left him speechless.

At that time, the information society was only in its infancy. Professional journals described the spectacular progress which we were going to make thanks to the new tools at our disposal. Most of us were aware that these developments were inevitable, but many continued to act as if nothing had changed. Paper still remained the most common repository of information.

Today, my laptop computer with its small monitor is a museum piece. It has been replaced by the electronic book. The reader can flip through the digital pages,[2] a series of electronic screens to which one can add, from anywhere in the world, such information, sound and images as one pleases. Virtual seminars are the order of the day, and business trips are not as frequent as they used to be; people mostly travel for leisure purposes. I myself have only come to Beijing to revisit the temples I saw 20 years ago.

We have all changed a lot, including those who at the time were afraid of the future. The much-vaunted 'globalization' of the last century makes us smile today; present-day historians hardly refer to it. Other deep changes, taking place almost imperceptibly, have transformed the world much more profoundly. On the other hand, despite the gigantic changes that have taken place since the turn of the century, much still remains to be done: inequality, unemployment, ecological disasters… none of these problems have been solved.

And yet, the key to the future remains the same: we must reveal the essential questions of the time and implement new solutions before other, and irreversible, consequences impose themselves on us to our detriment and, in the final analysis, render us obsolete.

Notes

1. Next Generation Internet: project aimed at renewing the Internet launched at the end of the 20th century.
2. The Media Lab, directed by Nicholas Negroponte, has been working since the beginning of the 1990s on this idea of permanently rewritable electronic paper.

Part I
Have We Become Obsolete?

Here we are, then, surprised right in the middle of our quantum leap. Caught between a future world of networking, electronic neighbourhoods and a silicon solidarity which reaches to the ends of the earth, and the all too present past, comfortably corseted in its corporate structures and hierarchies. These latter, seemingly ineradicable, are now collapsing about us, often burying in their fall those whom they previously sheltered and protected, while the former are not yet in a position to shelter those who seek refuge in them. So, we hesitate on the threshold, no longer sure of the route to follow.

Have we become obsolete? We have remained men of marble,[1] the products of Taylorism, with a predictable present and a foreseeable future, although we dream of being knights in armour, shining pioneers of the world of networking to come. Companies, the first global bodies, are advancing along this new path, often sloughing off those men and women who formerly helped to assure their success. At the same time, little remains of these successes but the aftertaste of the profits made; the pleasure of achieving things together has quietly receded into the background.

Not that progress has ground to a halt, quite the contrary. It is surfing the Internet, cloning and miniaturizing at an alarming rate, but it no longer brings happiness in its wake. In the past it was the faithful servant of society, assuaging the burden of our daily existence; today, many suspect it of having turned against society in an unholy alliance with the power of money. At the same time, society itself is making its own. Everything is going better, and yet everything is going badly.

1

Time is accelerating, space is widening, and contacts are multiplying on a worldwide scale, whether in a spectacular manner or in a harmless, everyday fashion. These three changes, discreet and yet sweeping, have given birth to a process of globalization which makes us afraid because we are still in the front line: the world is opening up and the Welfare State can no longer protect us within its boundaries; our social systems have been caught on the wrong foot by the competition.

We have to change without delay. 'Why change?' is no longer a relevant question. 'How to change?' is what concerns us now; how are we to come out of this uncomfortable quantum leap to which we seem to be condemned? Travellers between two worlds, should we perhaps lie as Christopher Columbus did when he falsely counted the days so as not to upset his crew? Or should we rather use our eyes to scour the horizon, scanning the skies in search of birds and the sea for debris, certain signs of approaching land? No doubt we should, and we should perhaps accept the fact that we are on a voyage, this painful passage between the past and the future which will teach us how to become.

Knowing how to become. This is a faculty which we all possess, perhaps more than we dare acknowledge. Engulfed by the deluge of changes in progress, we have forgotten what we have previously accomplished and assimilated. Let us take a look, for example, at what we have become in such a short space of time.

Information insinuates every instant of our daily lives. Travellers in the wild and sports fishermen are equipped with GPS,[2] students surf the Internet, truck drivers are linked to their firms via satellite. Using these tools to the best advantage is a strategy adopted by craftsmen who make violins as much as by international oil companies. Every day, there are more and more of us who work over long distances, serving our customers in the four corners of the world, teaming up with other nationalities, speaking other languages.

The intelligence and knowledge possessed by people, multiplied and magnified by these new tools, constitute the riches of those companies that have progressed further in 3 years than their traditional competitors would have done in 30. Banks without counters, but provided with sophisticated telephone and information networks, are at the service of their customers, wherever they are, 24 hours a day. Bookshops, insurance companies, car retailers and all kinds of associations set up their shop windows, and offer their products, their services and their know-how on the Internet. Intelligence becomes for these companies a form of strategic capital which they cultivate, store, measure and put a figure on in their returns.

Once a myth, now the prevailing fashion, today the electronic network is a necessity. This is why most organizations, public as well as private, seek to set up networks. Small companies pool their resources, their information and their employees in order to improve the services they offer and conquer new markets. The largest companies are determined to pull down their institutional pyramids and replace them by complex networks embracing the world, networks thus brought closer to customers made more choosy and fickle by the choices available to them on the competitive market.

Some of us already move effortlessly within this revolution, with its information, networking and sophisticated tools. Others turn up their noses as yet, convinced that it is all but a passing fancy. However, we are all aware that our days are numbered; other new revolutions are upon us. Their contours are as yet unclear, but their size is formidable; they will present huge and unavoidable challenges.

The same is true of globalization, and its entourage of dreams and uncertainties with which it fills our minds. It destroys even the most solidly established jobs and trades, while at the same time creating new ones. It blows the traditional organization of companies wide open. Some are able to re-form in strange, virtual and flexible patterns, the efficacy of which already impresses us; others collapse in ruins, destabilizing those societies and nations for which they were previously a source of wealth. Indeed, it seems to question the very value of our labour. Once, work enriched and cemented the wealth of societies; today it is but a piece of merchandise sold to the highest bidder on the global markets.

In the first part of this book we will concentrate on these new challenges and the forces which feed them. Some of these are familiar to us, others are unfamiliar, and will surprise us. From there we shall proceed to practice, to the companies: the confluence of technology, the riches of the economy, and of society with its variety of differences. The company is an essential locus in society, but must not be confused with society and is no substitute for it. This locus is strong when its efficiency is built upon the cohesion and knowledge of those it gathers to it, but fragile when cohesion collapses and knowledge runs out. The company is at the heart of the quantum leap.

Whether they adapt themselves or stumble in the attempt, companies are rich and laden with human resources, with projects or with regrets. Whether they make the leap without effort, or struggle to survive, all are aware of the stakes, and the majority already possess the necessary tools. All that remains is for them to become true 'hypertext' companies.

Notes

1. The men of marble were born on the planet Taylor, named after the inventor of a scientific method of organizing work. This was a solid planet, peopled by solid companies constructed of bricks and mortar in the form of pyramids. Life there was peaceful: change was not the torrent to which we are exposed today, but a slow-moving and quite predictable river. The man of marble had one trade and one life: to learn, work and wait for retirement. Cf. Jacques Chaize, *La Porte du changement s'ouvre de l'intérieur*, Paris, Calmann-Lévy, 1992.
2. Global Positioning System; an electronic compass, using a network of satellites to establish a position anywhere in the world to within a few metres.

1 The Death Mask of Narcissus

WORLD

The western powers that assure their workers a high standard of living ought to enter into some sort of agreement regarding the dumping of Asian manual labour, dumping which constitutes an imminent social and economic peril.

Raymond Patrenôtre,[1] 1934

Narcissus, the son of the river god, Cephissus, died because he fell in love with his own image, reflected in water but forever beyond his reach. Tiresias the soothsayer had predicted to Narcissus' mother, the nymph Liriope, that her son would live as long as he never saw his own face.

Like a carefree Narcissus, we have established our model throughout the world, and our economic system has become the rule. Today, though, it has come back to us as a competitor, and the face returned to us has become a death mask. Narcissus is worried; we would like to believe that it is the face of another.

The adolescence of the world

We are obsessed by globalization. It occupies our thoughts, heats up our discussions and, apparently dictating the strategies of nations and of companies, abandons in the street those discarded by the transfer of production from place to place. It draws us together, opening its networks to those eager to learn more about the world, and to minorities intensely protective of their differences. And yet it divides us: some see this planetary convergence as a promise of unlimited growth, of prosperity and democracy. Others prophesy social disintegration and

5

unemployment, strongly defending the right to retain, or to rediscover, differences of identity, culture and nationality. The former, marching behind the colourful and triumphant banners of global products, look forward with relish to the coming victory of 'syntegrism',[2] the new religion of universal sameness. The latter are preparing to defend every minute item of difference, even to the extent of total exclusivism.

Whether smiling or grimacing, the face of globalization which has been returned to us is none other than our own. Above and beyond conflicts of ideas and ideologies, the struggle faced by Narcissus is perhaps no more than an adolescent crisis. For the first time in history, the idea of the world is not just a dream, but a living image. For almost a generation now, the media have been relentlessly projecting an instantaneous and living image of the planet and its inhabitants. The new tools of communication have constructed a virtual nervous system which enables us to perceive humanity as a unity. For the first time, our own image and the image we have of the world coincide, and this fusion is both painful and contradictory. Our media-based nervous system is rapidly forming, and our planetary body is taking shape, ungainly and gauche at first, capable, like an adolescent, of unpredictable movements, gentle or brutal, barbaric or full of solidarity.

Like an adolescent searching for an identity, as we are gradually born into the world, the world becomes conscious of itself. Like a clear-sighted Narcissus, we have become spectators and actors, living through and yet observing the passing of our fragmented worlds, as they crack apart and lose their fixed points of reference, while the world of fusion and cohesion to come cannot yet be perceived. We already know that this transition is too rapid for some, while others, impatient, would like it to move faster. We are also aware that its advances will be followed by brutal reverses, as indeed was the case at the beginning of the 20th century.

A feeling of déjà vu

As a matter of fact, globalization is not a new phenomenon. Since the beginning of our world, from the Bronze Age to Marco Polo, the slow migration, at the pace of camels or horses, of objects, ideas and people, following the salt, tin and silk roads, patiently wove the network of links that connect us today. But it was not until the arrival of trains and steamships at the end of the 19th century that globalization first really made its mark on history.

This first phase of globalization, like the one in process today, was born of the freedom of trade and the explosion of new technologies. The thoroughfares of that time were not virtual, but were those of shipping and rail. At sea, the Suez Canal, opened in 1869, reduced the distance between Bombay and London by more than half; the same was true of the San Francisco–New York route after the cutting of the Panama Canal. At the same time, with the arrival of steam, the speed, power and tonnage of ships increased by leaps and bounds. On land, the development of the railway made it possible to link even the most distant regions: Canada was crossed in 1886, and the Trans-Siberian railway reached Vladivostok in 1904.

International trade tripled in volume between 1870 and 1914, a development which seemed so powerful it was thought to be irreversible. Sir Norman Angell, winner of the Nobel Peace Prize and the troubadour of the first globalization, wrote as follows in 1910: 'Today, international finances are to such a degree linked to commerce and industry that military power and politics are, in effect, rendered powerless. The rapidity of communications, which has made international credit, already in a delicate balance, enormously more complex, confers on present problems of international politics an aspect profoundly and essentially different from those of the past.'[3] Four years later, the nature of this peaceful development was radically altered, being replaced by global wars, both hot and cold. This 'parenthesis' was due to last almost 80 years: 'The international trade of the industrialized nations in proportion to their production reached 12.9% in 1913; in 1938 it had fallen to 6.2%, from which point it rose almost continuously to reach 14.3% in 1993...'[4]

Stationary emigrants

The first phase of globalization was European, with London as its centre. People moved in large numbers, travellers some of them, but mostly migrants, either to conquer new colonial territory or simply to look for a means of subsistence. Between 1870 and 1915, some 36 million people left Europe, two-thirds of them for the USA.

Today, the flow of capital and of information has surpassed the movement of goods and of people; more people travel as tourists than as emigrants. In this way, the process of globalization continues, making 'stationary emigrants' of us all. We no longer venture out to meet the world as in the last century; today, the world comes to live with us. Frontiers disappear, territories open up, traditional barriers have been removed; States and institutions have overflowed their boundaries. We are leaving the closed world of yesteryear, but without moving.

At the same time, we are all concerned about what is happening, no matter what our status or business. Globalization transforms people before institutions. Some see in this the opportunity to learn more quickly or live more intensely. In the past it was a question of travelling from town to town in search of a certain learned professor, or to track down a copy of some rare book which could open up a world of knowledge – today, a simple click of the mouse and, hey presto, you can be listening to a university professor at the other end of the world. Put in a CD-ROM, and the thousands of pages it contains replace distant and inaccessible libraries. Others suffer in silence the clamorous attack on this new omnipresent culture, without understanding it or knowing what to do about it. For all of us, globalization is no longer a voyage to a far-off place, but a profound mutation of our deepest roots, reaching down into the most intimate recesses of our personalities.

The roots of globalization

The process of globalization, whether as an ancient or modern phenomenon, is always activated by three levers: the development of cheaper and cheaper means of transport, the instantaneous transmission of information, and the fluid state of open markets. Today, as in the 19th century, there are three forces, three basic mutations, which move these levers. I have identified these in a previous work.[5] The force they exert is immense, and it would be useful at this point to recall them and follow their recent progress.

The end of the vertical world

The first mutation is that of space. In effect, distances have been abolished. Soon, no difference will be made between a local and a long-distance telephone call; both will be using the same satellite network. In 1998, for instance, thanks to 66 Iridium satellites orbiting at a height of 780 km, a local call travelled 1,560 km to reach its destination. In the next 10 years, some 2,000 new communication satellites will be dotted round in space, opening up a myriad possibilities for contacts by phone, video-conferencing and high-speed Internet access. That half of humanity which at present is deprived of the telephone because of the lack of infrastructure, in remote rural areas of China or India, will be able to communicate relatively cheaply.

The global market, previously partitioned behind customs and political boundaries, is increasing by more than 50% a year: experts[6] estimate that it will increase from 4 trillion dollars in 1995 to 21 trillion dollars in 2001! The world has become more open, but the centre of gravity has been moved towards Asia. In 1995, the OECD countries accounted for 57% of the global economy. The World Bank predicts that this figure will fall to around 45% in the year 2020.

The Panama Canal, a witness to the first wave of globalization in the 19th century, is today one of the symbols of this shift. Built by the Americans, it was returned to Panama on 31 December 1999. Saturated with traffic and unable to transport massive cargo vessels, it will face stiff competition from numerous projects initiated or maintained by Asian countries. Such, for example, is the project of creating a 'dry' canal in Nicaragua, launched by Samsung, Sumimoto and China Merchant Holdings. They envisage the construction of two deep-water ports on each side of the isthmus, connected by an express railway.[7]

Political geography follows rather than precedes the globalization of communications. The spectacular fall of the Berlin Wall opened up the sudden vision of a world without barriers, a single, free territory to be crossed at will by the triumphant hordes of modernity. In order better to profit from these new transverse currents, many countries have regrouped to form commercial regions. The countries of the Triad, prototypes of globalization in the 1980s, find today that new commercial groupings consisting of the most dynamic emerging countries are snapping at their heels. Customs dues and other import restrictions are rapidly disappearing. Not all the walls have yet fallen, however: some 80 countries are still waiting at the side of the road. Moreover, instances of nationalism or particularism which had been forgotten or ignored have reappeared on the scene. New walls are being raised, marking the boundaries between on the one hand a mobile world of free travel open to those who have mastered this new spatial freedom, its norms and its discourses, its highways and means of propulsion, and on the other a more static world which is developing new autarchies or seeking new directions altogether. Some people are already talking of the new Middle Ages.[8] At all events, this is a disquieting step forward within the new framework of open space.

The globalization of space is under way, but progress is uneven. Its preferred field of battle remains the economy, and its chariots are the company and the market. For the main contestants in the economic struggle, globalization is first and foremost a strategy. Multinational concerns are gradually becoming global. Companies which were once local are beginning to divide the world into zones, and feel at home there; small or large, water-supply companies, bakers, caterers, craftsmen or high-tech enterprises, all have come to understand the necessity of doing their business well in order to export their products. Whether by choice or under duress, employees and the managers of companies are setting out along this new path; their careers cover a range of territories, involving daily travel or prolonged stays abroad. Ten years ago, Danone only counted a few executives outside France; today, they have several hundreds, and more than 60% of the company's employees work outside France.

However, even though companies are becoming globalized, their customers remain local. Social globalization is advancing inexorably at a steady pace, striving to conquer the people of the future, especially teenagers. Whether the banners beneath which they rally are MTV, McDonald's, Lévi-Strauss or Mickey Mouse, what they have to do above all in common is to master, or at least utilize, the new tools of communication. Another tool of globalization, the Internet, is not only a place for the exchange of information. It is also increasingly a social arena where people can find their peers: the intense, closed circles of the intellectual elites, of film experts, surgeons, consultants, and university alumni; masquerades and personal contacts in 'Geo-cities'; single-parent mothers looking for advice on the education of their children, amateurs looking for gardening tips... the global tribes born of these contacts are only in their infancy. The networks are there in order to cement the bonds which will create added value, social in nature, but virtual.

The mutation of space abolishes distances, sometimes to the point of anguish. A whole planet hooked by the media watches a hostage drama with bated breath. The handclasp of deadly enemies now reconciled, in front of the cameras on a lawn in Washington, brings to our eyes those tears once reserved for our neighbours, now left to stew in their solitude.

Curiously enough, though, at the same time as space expands and becomes virtual, the growth of urban concentrations, far from diminishing, is accelerating. In 1900, the largest city in the world at the time, London, had 6 million inhabitants. In 1960, New York topped the list with 12 million. In the year 2000, Mexico City will probably be the largest metropolis in the world, with some 31 million inhabitants. In 1900, one person in ten lived in a town, as opposed to one in two in 1994.[9] Urban dwellers, who will soon form the majority of the world population, will live in megalopolies with millions or tens of millions of inhabitants. It would not be wrong to say that managing such cities will be the major headache of the 21st century.[10] The city, concentrated in space, is saturated space; the city, traditional meeting place, has become more and more often a conglomeration of ghettos; the city, which saves time by gathering all services within our reach, is becoming smothered under piles of debris. The urgent task at hand is to manage space, before the gates of the prison of time slam shut in our faces.

The new prison of time

We are short of time, and yet our life expectation increased by more than 30 years in the course of the 20th century, and our leisure time has tripled since 1900.

We are short of time because simultaneous time has become the rule. Information technologies have created a planetary time which is instantaneous and common to all. This is the second basic mutation. For more than 10 years now, CNN or the 24-hour radio station have supplied us with the same news, at the same instant, all over the world. The Paris Stock Exchange reacts the very same day to fluctuations on Wall Street, or the next day at the very latest. In 1929 it took three years for the American crisis to reach Europe. In terms of time, speed makes things easier and saves us money. Thanks to high-speed trains and fast computers we only need a few moments to accomplish things that previously took days. Speed makes a mockery of space: in fact no place is inaccessible any more, but while making a mockery of space it has closed the doors of the prison of time. In former times, the rich led a life of leisure; today, they have hardly a minute to them-selves. In the same way, in former times the poor lived a life of drudgery; today many of them, unemployed, do not know what to do with their time.

The lack of time has become an outward sign of success. For a long period of time, place was the essential factor: one belonged to this country, to that village or hamlet. Territory was the primary bond. Time unfolded its shroud at a measured pace, following the rhythm of seasons, of festivals, the hours linked to the bells of churches or the clock towers of civil institutions. Today, place no longer binds us, but new bonds create a new place, virtual in terms of space, but real enough in our minds: shared time has become the social bond par excellence. Time spent at work, with the family, with friends, at our hobbies… in this way the rites of the new tribes are constructed – a common time which unites hearts and minds at the places where they meet.

To be able to be linked at any moment, to be able to communicate at every instant, this is to be part of the tribe. The territory of each one is his or her own time. Look at the business tribe: from Tokyo to New York one day on the Stock Exchange lasts 24 hours, but a week is only 5 days. Five days of travelling around the world, from Singapore to Buenos Aires, before going home for the weekend. This also applies to the company, a virtual tribe more and more spread out in terms of space, and yet concentrated within the tension of time: budgetary and planning rites, the rhythms of strategies and forward thinking. These new tribes have their watchmakers, too, such as Gorgy Timing.[11] This is a small company in Grenoble which has set out to conquer the world by synchronizing, to the exact nanosecond, the ballet of train timetables, plane schedules and satellites. Speed has become a major strategic tool. Five years ago, it took 60 months to design and put a new car on the market; today, 25 months is enough. Time constructs a common culture.

Look, too, at the affective tribe constituted by family and friends, which takes over when the time spent on commerce is over. E-mail and telephone conversations take place outside working hours, when traffic is at its lowest. The space occupied by this tribe has also grown to fit a worldwide scale: Christmas in a family in the Antilles, and a game of bridge played over the Internet, bringing the players together across the time zones. Whether they meet in railway stations, at airports or on the Web, these tribes assemble without seeing each other, and without seeing those who do not relate to any of the members, those excluded by time. The stranger is no longer the person who is simply not here, but also increasingly the person who is not on the air at the time. The airspace of time is the present, the now, available at the click of a mouse button or by mobile phone. Formerly, the present moved slowly and predictably forwards. Only the future was uncertain. To master it, one had to learn to anticipate what was to come.

Nowadays, the future does not seem to interest anyone. There is too much to do in the present, which has become more and more unforeseeable, rich in choices and multiple contacts, seductive and dangerous.

We are short of time because the choices facing us have multiplied; we should like to make use of all the possibilities which we are offered. This is why, as customers, we increasingly refuse to wait, and want to have available, instantly, in real time, the products or services which we desire.

The frontier of trade and contact

Contacts between people, the exchange of goods and ideas, are expanding, but the nature of the process has changed. This is the third basic mutation. Today, globalization is not based on geography, as in the past, but on the specialization of companies.

In 1750, China and India represented 70% of the world production of manufactured goods, as opposed to the 20% covered by the 20 or so countries considered to be industrial today. On the eve of the First World War, the proportions had been reversed: India and China only represented a meagre 8% as opposed to the 80% covered by the industrialized nations.[12] England, the first nation to be industrialized, needed outlets and markets, not competitors, and in this way India lost its nascent industrial talents to become a captive market of the British Empire.[13] In America, apart from the abolition of slavery, the Civil War originated in the desire of the North to open up the South as a market for its industrial products, instead of the English products preferred by the Southerners.

Thirty years ago, half of the volume of international trade was accounted for by goods connected with agriculture, mining and energy.[14] Today, these sectors only account for 25%, the majority sectors being manufactured goods and services. Moreover, from imports to exports, the products are the same. There is only one, single global market. Finally, an increasing part of international trade consists of internal trading between different sections of the same company.[15] Relying heavily on the global market, the Asian countries are competing with us across the whole range of products: the percentage of manufactured goods among the flow of exports from developing countries rose from 20% in 1970 to 60% in 1990.[16] We no longer have the monopoly on any type of product. The places where things are made constantly shift due to the movement or concentration of production, while at the same time the market place of ideas collects in any given place the totality of the global market.

The fact is that ideas are propagated better and more quickly than objects can be moved. No more than 50 years ago, globalization was still linked to territory, land and the possession of place in general. Now, the globalization of knowledge makes a mockery of spatial considerations; information technology enables knowledge to cross the planet in an instant. Ideas meet, scornful of distance. On the other hand it is easier to trade in objects than in ideas. Formerly, one had to know how to extract riches from a place; now, riches have to be created by trade. It is no longer a question of conquering the world, but of constantly travelling across it.

The more the tools of exchange proliferate, the more we use them to zap from one virtual place to another, whatever the tribal time is at the moment. Companies have never encompassed so many different cultures, and yet in general communication appears to be more diffi-cult. Cultures and structures do not make good bedfellows: we wish to communicate over great distances, but have forgotten how to talk to our neighbour, whether across the garden hedge or at work. A sombre picture can be painted of a series of formal contacts in which the indi-vidual, defiant, almost autistic, attempts to recreate the distance which the modern world has abolished. We prefer to tire ourselves out with travel, burning up our time to avoid personal contacts. We draw back as soon as the mutation of trade and contact reaches down into our sphere of intimacy, precisely because contact involves both giving and receiving. Men and their companies live in a world of fusions and take-overs, of alliances made and broken. It will always be easier to bring objects and machines together than to bring people together.

Despite our resistance, however, these three mutations continue to make their mark. They are transforming the world, throwing up new landmarks and levelling others. New rivers flood the plain, while others dry up... a new landscape is under construction. Nowhere is this process more clear than within the company.

A world become global: the company

The company is one of the leading actors in the process of globalization. The opening up of space has made it possible to create a world-wide market, and the compression of time has placed the traders in this new market within the tension of the same virtual 'now' – all of which creates new opportunities to increase the rate of trade and contacts. In view of this, the company has become the first truly global social unit.

Companies become global as a result of the three basic mutations which are transforming our working lives. Increased competition and rapid innovations have reduced the life-cycle of industrial products: to make a profit you have to gain faster access to a wider market; to outdistance your competitors, you have to conquer new or distant markets before they do.

If it is true that in 1996 globalization only affected some 3% of industrial employees, today this figure is accelerating in a very tangible way. Even though the idea of a global community is still a rhetorical figure for most of us, companies are the spearhead of this development, but they are not alone: non-governmental organizations (NGOs) are moving with them or even before them, along this difficult and uncertain road. They are staking their claims to the political land as yet under development, whereas companies, for their part, are moving in economic space, where there is as yet more elbow room.

From classical theatre to space opera

The three mutations have completely broken the old 'three unities' rule of the classical theatre: the unity of time, space and action. In the case of the employee, the unity of action meant having only one boss. Today, the real boss often lives far away from those in his hire, at a distance which is often useful if problems arise. His teams have become increasingly autonomous, and are able to work without a direct leader. At one time, unity of action was related to following one particular trade; today, projects of varying design and length draw on people with increasingly diverse skills and competence. In many cases, the traditional boss is a figure of the past, and at the same time many people who were formerly employees are now working for themselves: 12% in France, 27% in Britain and 29% in Italy.[17] It is a question of knowing how to develop evolving skills, and to put them at the service of the increasingly volatile range of tasks called for by customers whose demands are strident and varied.

In former times, there was a unity of place: people worked for the same company all their lives, and the company itself did not change. Today, it is a question of knowing how to change. And even if people do not change companies, companies themselves change: new shareholders, new activities.

Finally, the unity of time has disappeared: fixed hours of work have become flexible; time zones are the warp shooting through the weft of the company's daily activities. Time spent on reflection is becoming more important than time spent on doing things. New technologies have set up the weft of time outside the times of physical presence, almost to the point of absurdity.

Now that these rules of the classical theatre have been abandoned, companies have in a double sense become the centre of debate, both as money-spinners, creating riches more and more virtual in nature, and as social units. Whether they like it or not, companies have become instruments of progress, the place where new technologies and social structures meet. Since the birth of the Welfare State, companies have become the point of contact between most individuals and these structures, and are in the process of becoming the instrument of our globalization. The unity of place and the unity of time were a gauge of social stability. Today, the company as an institution is split between its commitment to the virtual world at the global level, and the responsibility it bears as a privileged social unit. The unity of action made for simple tasks, easily comprehended. Today, tasks are increasingly subtle and abstract, and increasingly the province of those employees who are able to manage the symbols and tools of the mind rather than the hand. It is difficult to plot the new road ahead, and the rules of *space opera* have not yet been written, but a few possible paths can be discerned.

International or global?

The company is beyond doubt the first global social object, but as such it is still largely at the prototype stage. In 1998, for example, more than 60% of the turnover of ABB, a model globalized company, was centred on Western Europe, and in general it is true that the most globalized companies are solidly anchored in the continent from which they originate. For Europeans, globalization means gaining a foothold in American and Asian markets. For Americans, it means consolidating in Europe and attacking Asian markets. For Asians, it means conquering the two major Asian markets, the Chinese and the Japanese. Having said this, however, the process of globalization is under way and seems to be accelerating rapidly, closely linked to external expansion. In the case of European companies, globalization poses a double challenge. With the arrival of the Euro in 1999, trading within the Community, hitherto seen as internationalization, has been reduced to the bread-and-butter level of regional trade, in that more than half of the economic activity of the EEC has in this way been removed from the so-called international scene.[18] A large number of companies will have to learn how to master both this new regional space which is Europe, and the immense market opened up by globalization.

No matter what their continent of origin, many companies are multinational, but as yet only a few are already global. Being multinational means having several sections scattered round the world in different countries, linked indirectly with each other through the company headquarters. Being global means setting up a global added-value chain which links the local sections directly to each other. The links in this chain are all equal, with no dominating link. Generally, the management team of an international company comes from the country where the firm has its headquarters, whereas a global company is run by leaders of various nationalities, who have often lived in several countries, and its administrators are from several continents. In fact, a truly global company has globalized its space, its time and its contacts – it has made the three basic mutations a reality!

The space which forms its market is the whole world, and its activities are organized around global tasks. When one of these tasks or activities proves not to have the stature to cover the immense expanse of this market, it is simply dropped. Running a global activity means being able to cope with the far-flung nature of the territory, while at the same time penetrating the far corners of the local market close at hand. A global company does not 'delocalize', that is, shift its activities to other localities, but 'localizes' them, in the sense that its products are aimed at the whole world and yet adapted to each particular market, with as much local colour and flavour as possible! Microsoft, for instance, has placed its service functions in Ireland in order to 'localize' its software in the languages and, above all, the cultures, of European countries. On the other hand, 'delocalization' is no indicator of globalization; many companies shift their production to another country in order to supply the domestic market with cheaper products. More companies buy in China or in Poland than sell there. Sometimes, too, 'delocalization' is more expensive than was imagined at the outset. This bitter realization often comes to companies attracted by the low cost of manual labour in certain countries. Their enthusiasm cools down after a few months or years, when they find themselves burdened with unexpected transport costs, overstocking due to delayed deliveries, and the high cost of maintaining expatriate engineers or managers.

The global company knows how to utilize simultaneous time, directly or deferred: every day more and more people are becoming adept at using telephone conferences, e-mail, video conferencing or working in groups at a distance. Working across time zones imposes new constraints and accelerates time, but also allows for contacts to be desynchronized. The tools of long-distance communication are becoming increasingly cheap and user-friendly, but all agree that in order to communicate properly it is necessary to meet from time to time.

Finally, the global company knows how to change. It knows how to make use of the talents of the various cultures of which it is composed with both humility and pride: the humility to listen to these cultures and respect their differences, and pride in joining them together. There seems to have been much progress in this area. What still remains to be done is to carefully assess alliances, with a view to take-overs, or to see which have become authentic co-operative ventures. High-technology companies have established new types of links with each other, somewhere between competition and complementary activities, which we shall analyse later on. This is not always the case with companies doing traditional types of activity on national markets. In order to master the planetary space which was previously closed, a global company has to know how to combine competition and co-operation; space can hardly be further enlarged, but the cake can, providing larger slices for all.

Local or global?

All companies are not called upon to straddle the world, but all, whether they like it or not, have become global. A local public works contractor joining an international group soon learns that the choice of investments to be made is now compared with the profitability of quarries in India or highway projects in Brazil. In order to attract tourists from all over the world, a small chain of hotels in the South of France was previously forced to use a number of major global reservation bureaux. Now it has discovered a global ally – the Internet – which has suddenly provided it with new customers who are faithful and more profitable. A further example is a car dealer who reverses the rules of the game: instead of being subject to the competitive interplay of his suppliers, he approaches manufacturers from all over the world and offers to supply them with a local outlet suited to their requirements, adapted to their image and their sales strategy. Once a customer, he has become a supplier of retail outlets. Another situation is that of a printing firm faced with stiff competition from Italian and Chinese printers, and which does not yet know what kind of services or new equipment will make the difference. Similarly, there is the case of the cleaning firm which has been approached by one of its major global competitors on the lookout for yet another niche in the market; should the local firm sell out, or continue on alone? Finally, we could take the example of a sweet manufacturer who is forced to close down: lacking any particular identity or know-how, too big to be local and too small to be European, it is dropped by a major retail chain which requires suppliers that can follow it to the far corners of Europe and of the world.

Privileged trades are a rarity today. Frontiers have disappeared and large gaps have been breached in the walls of privilege. The market is globalizing all companies, even the smallest, through their suppliers and their customers. New technologies, new commercial allies or competitors are forcing them to develop their line of business, or the way they run it. Each company is forced to cut a new route along the chain of added value which previously it controlled completely, protected by frontiers and other protective barriers. It is a question of finding those breaches which give access to new opportunities. The question is: in terms of this new quest, should one lead, or should one follow? Is it not better to make a profit at the local level than lose money on global ventures? In order to answer this, a number of preliminary questions have to be asked.

Is your line of business already big enough to fit the new globalized space? Have your distant competitors succeeded in crossing the frontiers and straddling continents? If your competitors resemble yourselves and are coming closer to you, you certainly still have the time to consider the question posed above and to choose a globalization strategy before others do it. This is the pioneer strategy. This is the way in which a number of medium-sized companies have developed, moving from the national market in the 1970s to a European market, and now aiming at the whole world. This is true in the case of Gallet,[19] for example, a company founded in 1860 that makes helmets for astronauts or firemen. The declared strategy of the company is to use a global strategy, with production facilities situated at the heart of the principal markets, from Châtillon-sur Chalaronne to Hanoi via Casablanca and Quebec, but with a global approach to research and development. The same applies to the Peltz company, founded in the heart of the Alps, now a global specialist in safety equipment, and familiar to mountaineers, potholers and other professionals of this kind.

On the other hand, if your line of business is already global, all that remains is to evaluate the competitive value of your company. You have to analyse its chain of values, from purchasing to aftersales service, including research, manufacture, marketing and sales. What links in this chain are going to change, to become global, or perhaps remain local, or become localized? Not everyone is able to compete with global rapid delivery companies like UPS or DHL, but to become their local ally by ensuring that their service reaches remote country regions might just be an ingenious idea. Without doubt you will have to abandon some of the lines of business which are part of the know-how of your company, and decide to concentrate on just some of them. For example, it might be difficult to compete with major global airlines, but becoming their indispensable local ally might well be a profitable proposition. This is the strategy adopted in France by Regional Airlines, and also that adopted by Mærsk Air, which has transformed the small airport of Billund in Denmark into a veritable crossroads for air traffic in northern Europe.

Should you accelerate or slow down your development? This is the last question you have to ask yourself, and the most important one. Are you in advance of the others along this road to globalization?

Perhaps you have reached your 'lack of competence threshold' as a local, regional, national or multinational company? On the other hand, if globalization is unavoidable, do you possess the resources and the time to build up your global network? If the answer to this is 'no', then it would be better to remain a local, regional or national company, nurturing or redeploying your niche activity, rather than a company desperately trying to grow without the necessary stature, skills or resources. The examples are legion of companies that have been caught by rising waters on their road towards globalization, in full vigour at one moment and threatened by death the next.

Having said that, betting has not closed yet. There are examples of antique dealers, a local trade if ever there was one, who have placed their collections of furniture and rare books on the Internet; viticulturists sell their wines in the same way, Venice its masks, Murano its vases. Other companies that have already achieved international status have decided to put down local roots in order to distribute their products themselves; previously unique, these products are now faced with competition from other similar and cheaper products from other sources. In a market where one product looks much like another, the only way to compete with the upstarts is in fact to ensure for oneself a privileged channel of distribution. There is, however, always the risk that a company may grow to global proportions but leave the people involved far behind. Is it perhaps the case that for a company to increase men must decrease? The company is virtual, man is local…

The new crisis and the new Eden

The process of globalization is only in its infancy. Companies have hardly begun to pay out their chains of added value on a world scale. Technology and the probable evolution of zones of exchange created by communities of nations are going to exacerbate this tendency. In our daily lives we all contribute to this process. Businessmen travel the world, their fixed idea the will to link up these chains of value; they mobilize all the means at their disposal – new tools of communication, new zones of free trade, the most sophisticated information networks. The ever-increasing number of tourists set off in search of the unusual, and yet expect to find, from Madrid to Ulan Bator, familiar standards of food and comfort. Along with their children, they both propagate and consume the mercantile culture of Disney, Adidas and Calvin Klein.

In themselves, too, the new tools we use help to make us global. It took about 100 years for the car to become the possession of the *common* man, and almost as long for the telephone, but television took less than 50 years to become something everyone has. No doubt less than 20 years will pass before mobile phones and the Internet will be available to the majority. The speed at which these new tools become integrated into daily life is accelerating, thanks to the microprocessor, a key element of new technology which plays the same role today as electricity did in the last century. Moreover, when some new tool calls for people to share it, the speed at which it becomes a collective possession is accelerated when the infrastructure is in place. This is true of the car, for example, which only really developed when roads were built, often financed, moreover, by the car manufacturers themselves. The same will apply to the new communication technologies with the arrival of satellite networks – the 'motorways' of the sky.

Some people see globalization as the dawning of a new age of crisis; others see it as a warranty of peace, and describe in impatient terms the return of the booming 1930s. Supporters of the crisis theory point out that no global structure will arise to control or regulate this development, which goes beyond the frontiers of national states. The apostles of the new booming 1930s point out for their part that all the conditions for a new boom are present: companies, disturbed at first by the arrival of the new technologies, have not been able to make full use of them yet. A number of potential new markets, in Eastern Europe or in Asia, were closed. Today, however, all the markets of the world are open, and the new 'circumnavigators' are inviting us to set out on the voyage.

Notes

1. *Voulons-nous sortir de la crise?*, Paris, Plon, 1934.
2. Neologism invented by the author.
3. Norman Angell, 'The Great Illusion', *The New Republic*, No. 368, November 1997.
4. *La Mondialisation au-delà des mythes*, Les Dossiers de l'Etat du Monde, Paris, La Découverte, 23 January 1997, p. 33.
5. Identified by the present authour in *La Porte du changement s'ouvre de l'intérieur,* Paris, Calmann-Lévy, 1992.
6. *McKinsey Quarterly*, No. 2, 'What's New about Globalization?', 1997.
7. *Asia*, Inc. May 1997.
8. Alain Minc, *Le Nouveau Moyen Age*, Paris, Gallimard, 1995.

9. '6 billion people', exhibition at the Musée de l'Homme, June 1997.
10. Source: *Futuribles International*, 1994.
11. www.gorgy-timing.fr.
12. 'Le travail et l'emploi au fil du temps', in *Le Travail dans vingt ans*, Commission Jean Boissonnat, Paris, Odile Jacob, 1995.
13. Daniel Cohen, *Richesses du monde, pauvreté des nations*, Paris, Flammarion, 1997, pp. 52–5.
14. Jean-Yves Carfantan, *L'Epreuve de la mondialisation*, Paris, Seuil, 1996, p. 42.
15. At the beginning of the 90s, the internal flow within non-financial 'delocalised' companies represented one-third of the external trading of western nations (862 billion dollars in 1992). In J.-Y. Carfantan, op. cit.
16. Daniel Cohen, op. cit., pp. 52–5.
17. Bernard Brunhes Consultant, *Négocier la flexibilité*, Paris, les Editions d'Organisations, 1997.
18. Bipe, *Horizon 2002, l'euro et les nouvelles conditions de la concurrence*, 1997.
19. www.gallet.fr.

Crowded Market Places and Silent Streets

CUSTOMERS

A society cannot stop producing, nor cease consuming.

Karl Marx[1]

The market place has become market space, a space which, moreover, is permanently open, day and night, wherever you live. All the world's customers do their shopping there, at any hour of the day or night. The virtual crowd moves silently through the shopping mall, carrying out instantaneous transactions in all the languages of the globe. Sellers of books, cars, apartments or music, cybernetic hawkers, all unfold on the Web their coloured signs, animated logos and seductive slogans. The street is empty but the crowds are there, at my Internet window.

Globalization, which began thousands of years ago, moves relentlessly forwards. Space, time and contacts of all kinds are becoming globalized, and this has two major consequences for all of us, although especially for companies.

The rules of the game have changed: in a space which is permanently and boundlessly open at all times, where transactions are instantaneous, customers are less captive than they ever were, and competition is more intense. Behind these facts, evident to all today, new strategies for 'capturing' customers are being concocted, and a new ecology of competition is developing.

Second, the content of the game is no longer the same. Information has become the predominant factor: sounds, images, movement, raw facts, sophisticated conclusions – every day, new ways are found of transmitting information in all its forms, and the ubiquity of it is radically transforming companies and society at large. An economy based on knowledge is taking shape, bringing into question even the most established of trades and the careers even of those most deeply involved in their work.

These two revolutions, which are taking place simultaneously, are attacking the traditional foundations on which companies are based.

The revolution in the market place

Not more than a few years ago, one could speak of captive markets and unique products. Companies prospered in the protective shadow of customs barriers, sheltered behind political, cultural and perhaps ideological frontiers. One of the talents required of top managers was the ability to use their influence in an era of price controls and national production norms. Car manufacturers, for example, could play on the fact that there was a waiting list for their products to make their scarcity a quality factor. As foreign competition was hardly a reality, customers bought locally and were satisfied with the service provided by 'indigenous' manufacturers. A few markets were international, but most were national.

Today, these protective barriers have disappeared, and norms have become global. Our formerly captive customers are now exposed to the strong winds of competition. No line of business seems to be sheltered from this storm: wide chains of distribution find their wares all over the world, offering competition to local manufacturers. Car manufacturers have almost run out of ideas to seduce the consumer. In the past they were conservative, even parsimonious, but today their production capacity greatly exceeds the demands of the market. The market is expanding, but the lines of connection are shorter. Amazon, one of the largest bookshops in the world, on the Internet, became in the course of just a few months a major force to be reckoned with in the publishing world. A jeans manufacturer, tempted by the adventure of direct sales, soon realized that it was jeopardizing traditional retail outlets, and made a sudden volte-face; without the intermediary of the retail shops prices were becoming too attractive. Other companies, whose market prices vary widely from one country to another, have come to fear that the combination of electronic sales and the Euro will erase these differences, and are trying to create new competitive models.

'Direct' customers are legion, but they make industry afraid. Formerly, the fact that markets were split up enabled companies to make their own laws, but today they no longer own the customers.

Opening up the markets intensifies competition. The extended market homogenizes products and services by the admission of economies on a new and different scale. The launching of a new CD by Michael Jackson, or of Windows 95 and 98, takes place simultaneously on all the world markets. Traditional barriers have been forgotten; all that matters is the customers, their age, their needs and their purchasing power. Differences in stages of development between nations do not count any more: millions of people in India or China are dollar million-aires and now form part of the market. Suppliers of luxuries accompany the new elites from Moscow to Shanghai. Fast-food chains supply the emerging middle classes. The number of McDonald's restaurants has become an indicator of development, and the local price of their hamburgers an index of the mean local purchasing power.

The differentiated market: even though products and services are increasingly being designed for a global market, at the same time they are being 'localized', that is, adapted to meet the varying needs of regions, and the habits and cultures of different types of clientele. For a long time now, producers of champagne have differentiated between bottles destined for Britain and those destined for Germany by adding more or less liqueur, and the taste of Coca-Cola varies according to country.

A global approach, or local colour – whatever the strategy adopted, one thing is clear: what counts is not the product, but the customer, who is now able to compare your products with similar products from all over the world. For this reason, it is up to the company to capture and keep its customers, both near and far, and in a sense this fact raises questions that affect the whole company.

The old style of organization is no longer suitable. For a long time it was determined by the product and the manufacturing process, in a context of national standards and protected markets. Today, like it or not, organization has to be adapted to the company's customers, their moods and the hours they keep. Moreover, as well as its organization, the very line of business of the company is brought into question; know-how is worth no more than what customers think of it. Confronted by a range of choice increasingly wider and with many competing products, they have formed their own selection criteria. Accordingly, the line of business of a company is not only based on know-how, and on the intrinsic value of the product and services offered, but also on the value as perceived by the customer to whom they are offered.

From the product to the customer

Morris Tabaksblat, former President of Unilever, has summarized the demise of the product in this way:

> Manufacturers are no longer able to impose their will on their customers. The era of *push selling* is definitively closed. Now, we are fairly and squarely installed in the era of *pull marketing*. It is no longer a question of knowing what we can sell the customer, but of what we can learn from customers about their needs and how we can help to satisfy them.[2]

When we observe the market, the first conclusion that imposes itself on us is that in effect our traditional marketing tools are ill adapted to this task. Taylorism and the mass-production industries created a kind of marketing that mirrored themselves: it was a question of having a good product, the right price, a suitable promotion campaign and of positioning the product within distribution networks. These '4 Ps' created the prosperity of the post-war growth years. Today, all this has changed; the product is important, but the person who buys it is more important. Customers no longer place blind faith in manufacturers and products, so the company must be able to 'visualize' the customer.

'Visualizing' means being able to put oneself in the customer's place, to stop thinking in terms of the price fixed by the distributor, but in terms of the use value of the product bought by the customer, that is, the real price which the use of the product represents for the customer. As consumers, we make such obvious judgements daily, but they become alien to us when we see them through the eyes of the supplier, the company. This is how we can explain the spectacular success of the Formula 1 hotels in France, which offer their customers comfort, peace and ease of access at low prices, without making them pay for restaurant or reception services which they can do without. 'Visualizing' also means seeing what the customer has not yet seen, or has not yet dreamed of. In addition, it means seeing those who are not yet your customers, but could become so. 'Visualizing' means being visible: 'Concentrating on one idea, one word, which defines the company in the minds of its customers',[3] this is the aim of product positioning strategies. Finally, 'visualizing' means being able to see several people in the one customer; this is the object of situational marketing: 'The consumer is not the same person, depending on the circumstances in which he buys or consumes products. One of the classic examples of this is the air traveller who reacts completely differently depending on whether he is travelling for his company or as a tourist.'[4] However, being able to visualize the customer is only the first step to trading with him; the next step is to set up a dialogue, since one-way messages no longer make sales.

Knowing how to close a sale means realizing that proximity and convenience are vital. Even the best product will not sell if it is inaccessible; people want it right beside them, within reach of the phone, the Minitel (in France) or the Internet. Moreover, once contact has been established, the transaction itself has to be easy and pleasant: 'easy to do business with', as the Americans say. These remarks may appear banal, but many companies have forgotten to observe them. They have remained lofty, remote, even haughty, and have glorified their products while forgetting their customers, who have bought their goods elsewhere.

In this way, the '4 Cs' are born:[5] the product gives way to the customer; the sales price to the cost of use; bilateral or interactive communication replaces one-way publicity; and the convenience of purchase becomes more important than the scientific arrangement of supermarket shelves. Today, knowing how to 'visualize' and how to close a sale form part of a company's basic tools of trade, and making good use of these skills will enable it to present its own uniqueness in the face of its competitors.

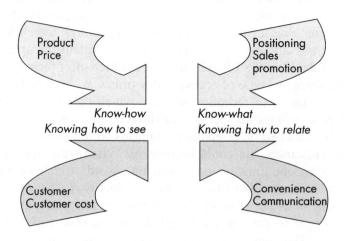

The death of competition, or competition to the death?

The fact is, competition is more fierce than it has ever been. The more classical marketing has changed, the more competition has evolved. At one and the same time we have seen side by side mammoth corporations competing with each other for size, and small, prosperous companies which have grown up around their feet, achieved adult status and then replaced them. Companies seek allies to present a common public image; they unite in order to offer their services in common. All these strategies, despite the fact that they are not new, are achieving greater importance day by day. On the scale of this immense world market, new competitive practices are being invented and deployed.

Observers of this development are divided. Some[6] see the resurgence of competition as a substitute for the old ideologies of confrontation; in this sense, heightened competition between companies or regions of the world is a substitute for previous ideological conflicts. Others[7] are eager to show that this competition to the death will indeed end up by killing off the protagonists and the system that nurtures them, like the well-known story of the fields of common pasture which, belonging to no one, were overgrazed by all. This is the fate of many companies that wear themselves out by fruitless and suicidal competition on shrivelled-up markets. Those who foresee the death of competition compare the competitive world to a natural ecosystem, the survival of which depends on opening it up rather than closing it in. Closed and protected systems are fragile, while systems that are open to fresh breezes from outside produce more resistant species.

Creating one's own viable ecosystem means accepting competition between the species that inhabit it, while foreseeing and organizing the internal renewal which will permit your company to gain advantage from it before all the others. We may use this image to understand the strategy pursued by Intel, world leader in the field of microprocessors: their microprocessors have been increased in power to meet the growing complexity and power of Microsoft software. The ecosystem thus created, nicknamed 'Wintel' (a contraction of Windows and Intel), has been flowering brilliantly for several years, but what will happen to this virtual ecological cycle if the complexity and power of new software stop developing? In order to avoid this disaster, the need for complexity and power has to be fed, its appetite constantly raised. This is what Andy Grove, when he was President of Intel, attempted by approaching the world of entertainment. He reasoned, not without cause, that microprocessors could be used in this world of diversion and images. His strategy is about to bear fruit: in the future there will be more PCs produced in the world than televisions. Microcomputers can decode films; you only have to connect them to the network and they become interactive, an old dream which television has never really been able to realize. A new ecosystem is under construction, in which the role of microprocessors will be decisive, and the role of Intel therefore doubtless reinforced![8]

Each must choose which of the two theses to subscribe to. The competition to the death thesis is usually linked to non-innovative strategies, content with the outcomes of the present situation. On the other hand, the creation of ecosystems idea is more often a characteristic of dynamic and inventive companies. Each of us plays a part in choosing between these scenarios, the choice of weapons to fight with and of the alliances which are to be formed, or, more often, abandoned.

The arrival of complementarity

The hut was filled with climbers and walkers. As night fell, the warden received a telephone call from a group of climbers trapped on a cliff face. Several volunteers came forward, ropes and lamps were quickly assembled. An hour later, the members of the lost group came through the door of the hut. When the time came to express their gratitude, one of the group proposed a toast to their rescuers, to the manufacturer of their mobile phone, and to the telephone company that had placed a relay on one of the neighbouring summits... a chain of value previously unknown, and which had saved their lives.

The intensity of competition has brought us to the point where we have forgotten the importance of complementarity. Strategic analyses often place the emphasis on competitors who may threaten the company's products, either traditional competitors or those which technical innovations may suddenly bring within the reach of the company's market. Using their existing customers' platform, water supply companies become competitors to telecommunication companies, soon to be threatened by electricity companies that transform electricity wires into telephone wires, television cables or Internet connections. The same analyses also put you on your guard against faithful suppliers who may often become dangerous rivals, seducing the customers you had made your own. Finally, they point out the risk you run of losing your customer simply because he has decided to make for himself the things you were supplying him with at considerable cost. Thus, many small printing firms have not resisted the massive onslaught of desktop publishing programs and colour printers. However, these analyses will generally not inform you of those who could complement you, the precious allies who will help you to develop and maintain the ecosystem which feeds you.

Today, complementary allies have become increasingly indispensable; the complexity of products calls for a wider and wider range of skills and knowledge. At the same time, the expansion of the market space, favourable to all kinds of links and alliances, places increasing demands on co-operation and creates the opportunity for it.

What is a complementary ally?

The customers of company A do not only buy the products of company A, but also the products of company B, which is complementary to A. A's products sell well because of B's products, and in fact could not do without them. Cars need petrol, but service stations have just as great a need for the car. Computers need programs, programs need computers. Complementary allies are often pursuing the same interests as yourself; they are sailing in the same boat. I like to see them as 'travelling companions'. As long as interests coincide, products are mutually supportive. It is nonetheless the case that new techniques, new approaches or whole new technologies can upset the established order and modify the relative influence of the complementary allies, or cause the routes followed by various travelling companions to diverge.[9]

Complementary and other allies are indispensable to companies wishing to develop and deploy new products in an increasingly large and increasingly demanding market. In order to find the complementary ally who will be able to move your company forwards, you have to look for the ally behind the belligerent, the opportunity for co-operation hidden behind routine indifference. Too many companies have but a narrow view of their customers, their suppliers and their competitors, a view fashioned by routine and the way they talk about them. In order to find an ally, one has to say to one's enemy or to those who are as yet an unknown quantity: 'What can we achieve together?'

The law of increasing returns

The latest development caused by the globalization of the market is the 'law of increasing returns', according to which technically superior products are overtaken by inferior products. The VHS system did not perform as well as Sony's Betamax system, but it has become the standard video system. In the same way, the Apple operating system was undoubtedly superior to the PC, but today it is marginalized. The law of increasing returns can be simply stated: our advantage over our competitors increases in proportion to the number of people who use our product. In the past, the reality was more usually the law of *diminishing* returns: the more our share of the market grew, the more difficult it was to increase it, simply because new competitors appeared who ended up offering a service equivalent to, or better than, ours.

Brian Arthur of the Santa Fe Institute, one of the specialists in and popularizers of the law of increasing returns, offers two examples of it, one older and one more recent. The QWERTY typewriter keyboard was invented to slow down the speed of typists rather than increase it, in order to make them more suited to the reduced performance of the first Remington typewriters. It became a standard simply because Remington had the largest number of typewriters in use. The same is true today of Microsoft, whose word processors and spreadsheets have 'cornered' the majority of computer uses. Having said this, DVD is well on the way to ousting VHS, and the Netscape browser and other Java programs once threatened the hegemony of Microsoft. The 'law of increasing returns' can explain a lot of successes in cases where companies have been able to create a new market and then dominate it.

Can this law be applied to your company? Certainly, if you are in the domain of high technology, the privileged realm of highly complex products. Certainly, too, if you have a franchise: the more McDonald's restaurants that are opened, the more the fame and power of the company expand. Whatever your area of activity, the more your products or services have a high intelligence or information content, the more the law of increasing returns will apply, for a reason which will be explained in detail later: information breeds when it is shared. In addition, the more you are able to make use of complementary allies who will help you to disseminate your product, the more this law will operate in your favour.

Having said this, being able to visualize the customer, to trade, to gain allies and disseminate products are of no use unless a company is able to create real and competitive added value out in the market space.

Value

Value. This is a term which has been overused and has today lost some of its significance.

Who is to judge the value of added value? Customers, of course, but they use their own criteria, and not those which their suppliers would have them use; shareholders do so increasingly, but their capital investments are diversified; employees, whose loyalty is no longer inherited, will create added value if they can see some of it coming their way and if the company recognizes their efforts; society, by virtue of the law and the pressure of lobbies, is the ultimate judge of added value. However, we must pay close attention to the facts: to a large extent added value is neither recognized nor purchased. This is certainly true of what we could call 'added social value'. Children spend many long years at school before reaching adulthood, the quality of relationships at work has improved, and reduced and more flexible working hours leave us more time to live our personal lives. Some day, perhaps, we ought to try and put a value on all this, but in the meantime, the only type of value that is measured is mercantile, the value of trade.

How is added value to be created today? By using a short-distance, direct approach, or a long-distance, more exclusive approach?

The short-distance, direct approach is based on proximity. Customers can be reached directly, without an intermediary, but at the same time they are looking for increasingly better, improved products. This is why alliances and complementary allies are important. Your customer, even though far away, can be reached over the Internet, but if your product has to be physically delivered, make sure to find some good allies – a delivery service that can ensure rapid transport, and a bank that will guarantee security of payment.

The long-distance, more exclusive approach. Your line of business is only of any value on a world scale. Your know-how has to learn how to travel, but before getting the show on the road you need to run a constant check on the best in the field in order to avoid the incursions of competitors who are also doing the world tour. And if you finally decide to go, make sure that you are able to survive the trip. The fact is that the opening-up of the global market, the development of information technologies, and perhaps most of all the convergence of cultures allow many local businesses not only to exist but to export. This applies, for example, to small businesses with a niche production, such as craftsmen or rare technological applications: a baker who knows how to make French bread in Tokyo, a cabinet maker in New York, a wine expert in China, a rare, specialist area of biotechnology or a foundry... in all these cases, the stakes are the same: possessing a certain know-how and customers who will buy it.

Having decided on the strategy, the trick is to put it into execution. Whether short or long, the chain of value which you are about to set up will be a complex assembly of objects and information, both physical and virtual.

In many cases, the production process has become almost banal, and transporting the finished product to the other side of the world is no longer expensive. On the other hand, being innovative, solving a production problem which has foiled your competitors, finding the cleverest and most viable method of production, knowing how to plan and monitor the transport of a particular product along a logistic chain that spans the world – these are all activities that create real added value, competitive value.

It is important to create this chain of competitive value, and to make sure that you keep control of it, so as not to lose any of the essential strategic links in the chain, to firmly establish and consolidate your business. And while we are on this point, what in fact is your business?

The term 'business'

'What is your business?' This was the question put by Peter Drucker to the directors of Service Master, a giant company offering cleaning services. 'House cleaning', answered one of them, 'garden maintenance', said others, or 'pest control and disinfection'. 'No', replied the famous consultant, 'your business is to train the least-skilled people and make them functional'. The fact is that many of the services offered by such a company are jobs which the customers do not want to do themselves.[9]

The directors of a large mail-order company asked themselves the same question.

> What is our business? Producing a catalogue, building up stocks, mastering all means of communication at any hour of the day or night... yes, this is true, but our principal task is to learn how to capture our core customer, the active woman. She sends her order to us at the beginning of the week, and expects delivery before Friday. If not, she will go to the large department stores, to shopping centres or traditional shops, which will therefore capture our business the following weekend. The basic skill required of us is to attract her attention and then be able to deliver speedily, at any time. Our essential allies here are the rapid delivery firms that can deliver anywhere in France, or in Europe, in the space of a few hours.

Here, in a few words, the directors of the company have made the essential point: our business is not what we choose, but what the customer decides it is, aided and abetted by our competitors. Our true business, therefore, is to create for the customer that chain of value that he or she is prepared to pay for.

The end of traditional businesses?

A scene along the banks of the Seine in the Middle Ages: three stone-masons are at work shaping a block of stone. A passing traveller asks them what they are doing. The first stonemason replies: 'I am shaping a piece of stone'; the second answers: 'I am building a wall'; but the third one says: 'I am building a cathedral'. This elegant definition of a trade, of the value added by the final aim of the activity, falls a bit short today: what use is a cathedral if there are no worshippers?

Where we in English use the words 'trade' or 'business', the French use the word *métier*, which is a typically French term. The Danes use the word *næringsliv*, cognate with the idea of 'nourishment' ('the 'nourishment of life'). But how is a trade or business to be defined? In terms of know-how, or know-what? In terms of visualizing or closing the sale? At all events, a trade is no more simply a question of know-how; it is both what you know how to do, and what your customer would like you to know.

Does your company perhaps still resemble a particular clothing company which was losing its market share: 'What is your business?', the directors were asked by the consultant called in by the worried shareholders. 'We make suits for men!' 'Suits for men!', retorted the consultant, 'Be thankful you are not still making frock-coats. Your business is not to make suits, but to dress men for specific places and occasions. This is what your competitors have understood, and it is their clothes that provide elegance and comfort to the lives of those customers whom you have lost.'

It is true, of course, that trades contribute to the creation of a work of art, whether clothes or cathedrals, but we must not delude ourselves into thinking that our trade belongs to us. It is our customers, our competitors, our suppliers and the market that decide whether it is to continue or not. There is a special kind of arbitrage taking place today at the global level. A trade is defined in relation to a customer; it is not a status quo, continuing for ever.

The globalization of the market and the arrival of new technologies are the two factors which combined have exploded the old idea of trades, and those who have sparked off this explosion are the main actors on the market: your customers, your suppliers, your competitors. All three can force you to go global. You have to follow them if you want to preserve your business, but in order to do it properly you must support it by new tools or new complementary allies. The effects of the explosion are felt all along the chain of value, affecting purchasing, aftersales service, research and development, marketing and the manufacturing process. Each stage of the added value process is being transformed. Some of these stages should become global. This is more and more often the case with research: the convergence of taste and norms and the change of scale which gives us access to a much greater market are leading companies on to think across previous boundaries in terms of the whole world. Other aspects, such as service and personal attention to the customer, will remain, or will again become, local.

It is possible to open the eyes of those who cannot visualize their customers, and to teach the taciturn to enter into a dialogue of exchange, but it is very difficult to describe the trade of those who have turned their business into a status quo.

Pragmatism or the status quo

There was a large French company, contractors doing public works, which decided to employ miners who were to be retrained for other work. Their skills were analysed, and the conclusion was that they were very close to those required by the trades involved in public works. However, many refused the offer of a job; the trade offered them seemed too different, less demanding and less dignified. The French have a reputation for turning their trade into a status quo. How many of us have made such a tight bond between skills and a particular trade, and between that trade and the status quo, that we have lost the ability to change?

This is no doubt because practising a trade means finding a balance between effort and comfort, between pain and pleasure. You have to make an effort to construct a product which will satisfy the customer, and then enjoy the comfort of the reputation you have made. You have to pass through the pain of apprenticeship before you can taste the pleasure of the trade you have mastered. But when the customers, your competitors and the other people who compose the market begin to call your trade into question – a trade which has become an instrument of social recognition, the status quo – then pain and effort drive away comfort and pleasure. Know-how is only one aspect of a trade, indissolubly linked to the will to succeed, to effort and pain. Without the will to succeed, a trade is but a motherless child; without know-how, the will to succeed is but a dream.

Globalization has opened up the market, upsetting traditional patterns of competition and questioning the competitive value of companies. Today, it challenges even the most established of trades. On the other hand, the market is not solely responsible for these upsets; for several years now, revolutions in the field of information technology have been eroding the basis on which the traditional strategies of many companies are based.

The knowledge revolution

The Gulf of Mexico, spring 1997. Texaco announces that oil wells that supposedly dried up in the 1970s are to be reopened. The American oil company has a program that can make three-dimensional diagrams of abandoned oil fields. A number of survey vessels equipped with seismic sonar equipment relay their data directly to the computers. The images obtained reveal that in fact only 30% of the capacity of these 'dried-up' oil fields has been exploited. Drawing on this information, the company decides to drill again. The drills, remote controlled from the surface, bore their tortuous path down to these deposits unknown to their predecessors, who were working in the dark. More than ever today, wealth is based on knowledge.

Millions of customers have chosen to entrust their money to banks without branches, accessible at any moment by phone. Books are sold on the Internet from bookshops with no books in stock. A rapid transport company and a telephone company exchange information. This enables the former to identify and canvass companies that make frequent calls to China, offering them a service adapted to this destination. Every day, new services are invented based on information, software, interactive contacts... elements of added value less and less physical, making a direct appeal to the use of intelligence.

The knowledge economy of information in action is gradually stealing a march on the economy of objects.

> In the course of the last three years, the high-technology sector has accounted for 27% of the gross national product [of the United States], compared to 14% for the construction sector and only 4% for the automobile industry. Last year [1996], an amazing 33% of the growth of the GNP came from the information technology industries, the Internet boom and the development of direct television satellites.[10]

The productivity of knowledge

Information, source of wealth, strategic tool – words used in so many contexts that they have lost their meaning. Information is added value in its own right. Have we really understood this?

Many managers still regard information and knowledge as luxuries, pleasant accessories, not directly connected with the real productivity of their company. 'True' productivity, they think, still comes from the machines, the shining metal sources of power. To admit that information and knowledge are essential to the enrichment of their company is a difficult step for them to take. To recognize and utilize the 'economizing'[11] properties of knowledge are as yet rare talents.

Here are a few arguments, then, with which to confront the sceptics. Are you prepared to neglect a tool which will reduce your stocks and improve your annual returns; which will avoid you having to build the new premises you think you need; a tool which, in fact, will make your competitors more effective?

The knowledge economy will reduce your stocks. For a long time, having lots of things in stock was the only way to satisfy customers. In this way one could provide them with the required product when and where they wanted it. A central storage place, therefore, with regional and local depots, provided the best possible service. If the product was not in stock, the customer was kept waiting. Today, though, customers are not kept waiting, and yet stocks have been reduced. In many cases, they have disappeared completely, gradually being replaced by a network of information. This network anticipates, registers and interprets the needs and commands of those who use it; it foresees what components are required, gets them ready, and delivers them 'just in time' for the production of the product in question, with no delay whatsoever, using some means of express transport. You no longer have objects in stock, instead you manage a flow of complex information which produces and delivers the product at the required place and time. For a long time it was thought that 'just-in-time' delivery only applied to the car industry, but, following the example of those computer suppliers who use state-of-the-art components to assemble the computer you have ordered over the Internet to suit your special needs, many companies, including some of the most traditional trades, are moving over to delivering 'fresh products'.

Finding a pair of shoes has become much easier today. In order to meet the challenge of competition from the emerging countries, Christian Pellet, a shoe manufacturer, can make and deliver the shoes of your dreams within 48 hours. Even better, Custom Foot invites its American customers to choose their Italian shoes from models available in their store in a variety of types of leather; the size is measured and checked by an electronic scanner which uses 670 measuring points. The order is passed on to the factories in Tuscany by modem and the shoes are delivered several days later, at a price very close to ready-to-wear products.[12]

When the product sold is pure information, it passes without intermediary from the producer to the customer. This is true of pay-films, which will soon be replacing stores that hire out video cassettes, or electronic newspapers which can already be read on one's laptop, or printed out at home. It might perhaps also be true one day of this book, which has followed a long road from the publisher to the bookshop, but which you will be able to read on-line at home, or print out for yourself.

The knowledge economy will improve your annual returns.[13] The new companies registered on the Nasdaq or the Nouveau Marché are striking examples of this development. If we compare them with traditional companies in terms of capital, their holdings of classical assets (buildings, machines, land) are ridiculously low, but their annual returns are moving in the same direction as the leading industrial companies in the world today. An American study of the leading industrial companies noted on the Stock Exchange revealed that in 1982 corporate assets represented more than 62% of the total value of the companies, compared to 38% in 1992.[14] Apart from these figures, further proof is furnished by the evidence we can see around us. In France in the traditional and highly visible banking sector, new companies such as Cortal and Banque Directe have replaced their stone facades and service counters by databases, telephone lines, and a 24-hour service.

The knowledge revolution increases the performance of your employees tenfold. We have already forgotten the amount of human energy required no less than 20 years ago to collect and sort information: the clacking of typewriters, carbon paper, stencils, ledgers, telegrams, telex, and so on – so many tools connected with information and communication, forgotten today, which then laboriously constructed the knowledge economy. Then, more time was spent collecting and sorting information than in dealing with it. Today, information is more or less available instantaneously, often pre-arranged by software growing more powerful day by day. All we have to do is use it, which means that company employees can use most of their intelligence doing just this, all the time. Such a revolution in the course of a few decades has radically transformed, or totally destroyed, the traditional sociology of these companies, a phenomenon which has been widely studied, especially by Robert Reich,[15] Secretary of Labor to Bill Clinton during his first term as President. He has identified three types of workers within this new economy: first, those who handle objects, routine factory or office workers, a dying breed; then the service workers, specialists in personal relationships, who are on the increase; and, finally, those who handle symbols, from consultants to engineers, who analyse situations and problems and who invent strategies or products. These people are the beneficiaries and the principal actors within this new knowledge economy.

However, despite all the riches that it has brought us, the knowledge revolution still has a long way to go. Many company directors, born before this revolution started, still confuse their business with the formal trappings that form the history of their companies. They mistake the container for the content, the external form for the substance, as did those leaders of the cleaning company to whom Peter Drucker was speaking (see above). Today, on the contrary, companies born into this knowledge economy perfectly reflect their line of business: Microsoft, which sells programming know-how, has no factories; Nike, Adidas and Reebok have developed communicative know-how and a capacity to manage those trend-setters that shape fashions, and have subcontracted the central parts, or indeed the whole of their production. Ten years ago, these companies were described as 'empty vessels' by observers whose sense of judgement had been dulled by the industrial era.

In effect, true trade is pure information, pure knowledge. To describe it properly one has to emphasize its content in terms of information, pure knowledge and applied knowledge. In order to keep renewing it we have to invest in the creation, the effectuation and the renewal of the basic knowledge on which it feeds. Most of all, this means understanding and mastering the three stages of the creation of value.

The three stages of value

Today, if you are going to master the chain of value which will build up and consolidate your business, you have to master the science of information. You have to know how to extract information and to assess its value. For a long time, we have concentrated on objects and the material conditions required to make them, which constituted the first chain of value – the physical chain – from the raw materials to the finished product. This chain will not disappear for a long time: it will always be necessary to buy, transport, transform, package and deliver material things.

However, to this chain of physical value has always been attached another, that of information. The first known written sources, the Sumerian tablets, were in effect ledgers, kept to register stocks of corn and livestock. They enabled people to 'see', engraved in the clay, the livestock and the reserves of food at their disposal. Information is the shadow cast by objects. Whereas in the past this shadow was, as it were, frozen in writing, today it follows the object: thanks to information technology it is possible to follow the evolution of an object at all times, from conception to sale. In other words, the physical chain is accompanied and controlled by its 'double', a chain of information which feeds on the physical chain, and which measures the time, direction and quality of the physical flow from the placing of an order to the delivery of the product. The information extracted, if properly used, facilitates control, accelerates the process, and identifies in real time where things might break down or go wrong. Information technology has made so much progress in terms of capturing in real time information in all its forms (weight, colour, appearance), that a NASA technician is able to use his computer mouse to control from the earth a small robot on the surface of Mars, 190 million kilometres away. At a more prosaic level, in order to concentrate on their essential trade, an increasing number of companies subcontract the physical chain in its entirety, content to follow and guide it along the right path with the help of the information extracted and processed in real time throughout the whole procedure.

However, if we take a closer look, this chain will often appear incomplete. The degree to which companies have integrated information is still very patchy, and this is a handicap for those that wish to become global, as they are unable to control all the links of this chain of value laid out across the world. It is also a handicap for those companies that have chosen to specialize in one of these links in the chain of value, as they are not able to communicate with their partners, who are the external links in the chain. This is the case, for example, of a certain company in the textile sector working on the just-in-time principle with a wide range of deliveries. However, because the company's software could not react quickly enough to sudden changes in product requirements, production had to be adjusted manually every day. The software had been designed several years earlier, before the just-in-time system had been invented and at a time when competition was not so fierce. Whether the links in the chain are internal or external, it is useful to have a clear picture of all of them, and to identify possible 'black holes': your production system might show you the situation of products being made at any given point in time, but strangely enough, once they have been dispatched no one knows where they are. Have they already been delivered, or are they lying on a quayside somewhere? Your commercial statistics can tell you everything about the past, but your databases are silent about future scenarios. In the same way, your accounts minutely record even the most banal expenses, but tell you nothing about added value!

Very often the chain of information is in place, but it is a veritable Tower of Babel. The main players in this second chain of value, usually people working with information technology, pull down these Towers of Babel to replace them with integrated systems. This market would doubtless never have existed if companies had built up their chain of information extraction with the same attention to detail with which, in the spirit of Taylorism, they had organized and streamlined the chain of physical production. If we are to remain competitive, there is a pressing need to replace and strengthen the missing links in this second chain. Moreover, in order to avoid past mistakes, it will be necessary constantly to adjust and modify it along with changes in organization or production processes. Indeed, we shall need to go further than this. The chain of value is no longer the enslaved shadow of the physical process; it has achieved its independence, and to an increasing degree it shapes this physical process, since any modification to the latter is directed by new programs of information technology. Every move made by a company derives from, or is virtually represented in, the information system: an obvious point, but one which is often ignored. How many attempts at much-needed reorgani-

THE THREE CHAINS OF VALUE

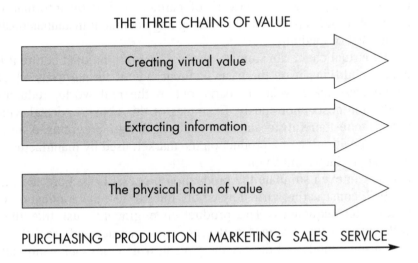

PURCHASING   PRODUCTION   MARKETING   SALES   SERVICE

zation have failed because the required information processes were not available, or distorted the original intentions?

It is even more important to master this virtual chain,[16] because it can in itself become a tool for the creation of value. The point is that when all the links in the chain of information have been assembled, one has a virtual reproduction of the whole chain of physical value. In this way, more added value can be created, as do those rapid transport companies that enable their customers to follow the progress of their packages in real time. This is also true of those companies that work with digital documents, plans and orders; those involved are never in contact with a physical document, plan or order, but they are nevertheless able to work in groups, to shape new products and meet orders in record time.

Creating a product on the basis of design studios spread throughout the world is already normal procedure for many companies. Moreover, each year tens of millions of drawings made by architects or engineers are sent by express courier, and other new services are at your disposal if you do not possess the equipment yourself: documents, drawings, photographs, X-rays or film rushes can be digitalized, sent by satellite and restored at their destination to the original medium, whether paper or whatever, without using any form of transport, at the same cost as traditional courier services and 24 hours faster. At least, this is what Dietzgen Advanced Technology Services are promising. This company set out to conquer this lucrative market in 1997, using a global network of partners linked by information technology and capable of reproducing any document instantaneously in any sort of medium.

The virtual chain can simulate the working of a product before it is made, modifying it on the basis of thousands of virtual trials which would have taken years to carry out in the real world, reducing production costs enormously. Examples of this abound: virtual wind tunnels to test aircraft fuselages or car body design; programs to simulate the positioning of a product on the market, used by manufacturers of food products, and so on.

One can even simulate the production process itself. Ford did this in 1997, constructing virtual assembly lines to test the application of production sequences. The production engineers, just like their colleagues in the design department, can construct and 'see' three-dimensional models of the assembly plant, which they can manipulate on their monitors just as if they were building a real car. Ford have calculated that the savings achieved by using such software run into hundreds of millions of dollars a year. Many of these programs are very expensive and developed to order in the greatest secrecy by those who are going to use them; others are available to all at reasonable cost.

One can actually go a step further. Not being content to make a virtual detour in order to create that added value which, in the end, will be the value of a physical product – be it a car, plane or a brand of yoghurt – one can remain in the virtual world and put a value on the information extracted itself. This is the third stage in the creation of value. One example of this is a chain of supermarkets which constantly registers the products sold in its outlets and then sells its databases to its suppliers, or to institutions that carry out opinion polls or monitor consumption. Another example would be an industrial concern that puts its digital catalogues at the service of its customers, or of engineers and construction departments elsewhere. These latter, from anywhere in the world and at any time, are able by the simple click of a mouse to integrate plans, data and pictures from this catalogue into the products which they then offer to their own customers. This is also rapidly becoming the case with sound and moving pictures, which, once digitalized, never leave the virtual world. Video cassettes, CDs and their enticing packaging will disappear, to be replaced by digital products downloaded directly to your television, stereo or computer.

Of course, some of the examples given here might seen ill-adapted to many of us. Our lines of business are different: we are after all neither Boeing nor Sony. At the same time, we know very well that the mastery of this chain of information and the fluid flexibility of this virtual chain will be great assets to our company – at the service of our business and of our clients. To innovate, to solve problems that confound our competitors – these are talents which today should find their expression not only along the familiar and visible chain of physical value, but also in this new, virtual world devoid of shape or size.

Whatever the road we choose to follow, whether virtual or physical, on the ground or in the market space, let us never lose sight of our customers. We shall have to get used to only having a virtual image of these customers – and many have already taken this step.

In order to manage this double chain, virtual and physical, it will often be necessary to transform the organization of our companies.

Notes

1. *Œuvres,* Editions La Pléiade, 1965, p. 1066, quoted by Fernand Braudel in *Les jeux de l'échange*, Paris, Armand Colin, 1979.
2. Amsterdam, speech made at a seminar organised by the International Advertising Association, 6 June 1997.
3. Jack Trout, *The New Positioning*, New York, McGraw-Hill, 1996.
4. Bernard Dubois, interview in *Marketing Magazine*, December 1997.
5. Robert Lautenborn, 'New Marketing Litany: 4P's Passé; C-Words TakeOver', *Advertising Age*, October 1990, p. 26.
6. Philippe Thureau-Mangin, *La Concurrence ou la mort*, Paris, Syros, 1995.
7. James F. Moore, *The Death of Competition*, New York, John Wiley & Sons, 1996.
8. *Fortune*, 17 February 1997.
9. Andrew Grove, *Only the Paranoid Survive*, New York, Currency Doubleday, 1996.
10. *Business Week*, 21 March 1997.
11. Manfred Mack, *Co-évolution, dynamique créatrice*, Paris, Village Mondial, 1997.
12. *Fortune*, 10 November 1997.
13. Cf. Thomas A. Stewart, *Intellectual Capital*, New York, Currency Doubleday, 1997.
14. Cf. Leif Edvinsson and Michael Malone, *Intellectual Capital*, New York, Harper Business, 1997.
15. Robert Reich, *The Work of Nations*, Random House, 1992 .
16. Jeffrey F. Rayport and John J. Sviokla, 'Exploiting the Virtual Value Chain', *Harvard Business Review*, Nov.–Dec. 1995.

The Company is Virtual – We are Not

ORGANIZATION

> To take up the challenges of tomorrow with the organizations of yesterday means exposing oneself to the problems of today.
>
> Hervé Sérieyx

Michel was one of the innumerable middlemen who appeared on the scene at the end of the 20th century and whose prosperity was linked to networking. His work consisted in identifying for customers the most competitive resources available. Having recently been contacted by a chain of restaurants that wanted some promotional T-shirts made as cheaply as possible, he had put together a package involving two months' production at a textile factory in Bangladesh, a couple of Russian designers and the services of a Genevan quality-control company, who also assured the security of money transfers within the network. In order to pinpoint the Bangladesh factory he had put out a request for tenders over the Internet, and had received almost 400 responses in the course of a few hours – from Palestine, Africa and even the Republic of Sicily. To get hold of the Russians he had made use of a second middleman specializing in design, who in turn had contacted his local agent. This had been an expensive process, but it was important that the new client should be satisfied. All three associates would work together without ever seeing each other. Each of them would carry out the task assigned to them, and then the temporary association would be dissolved.[1]

To summarize: more than ever, the importance of your product is to be found in your relation to the customer, in terms of service. The value which your business brings to the process is increasingly connected with information and relationships. So, in the face of this major revolution, what is the situation regarding your company organization? Is it still shaped by your products, or rather by this relationship with the customer involving feelings, information and the exchange of a lot of knowledge but very few physical objects? What are the characteristics of a company organization centred on the customer?

The four gateways of the network

Some people have already found the answer to the above question: organize it as a network! This is because a network, based most of all on relationships, is a flexible construction easily adapted to the needs of customers, whereas the classic Taylor-inspired chain of events leading to the transformation of objects is totally directed at the product, and is therefore, in this respect, blind. In order to be effective, the Taylor type of organization has to be programmed and organized, whereas a network manages on its own and quickly identifies the skills we ourselves lack, even at the other side of the world.

Today, the Taylor chain of events has become very complex: there are many more kinds of know-how to be mobilized, and they are more and more specific. Very often, this web of activities is not physical at all, and is spread out both in space and in time. In space, because know-how has to be collected on a global basis; in time, because today it is possible to keep digital stocks and then assemble at the required moment products constructed either in real or in staggered time.

On the other hand, this complex, virtual web is also fragile: one weak link in the set-up can endanger the efficiency of the whole. A perfect product delivered too late does not offer the kind of service required by a customer with deadlines to meet; a missing or defective part can break down the sophisticated systems of a rocket ready to launch. We have to combine the kind of reliability which builds confidence with a flexible attention to changing needs. This is the challenge which the network has to take up.

The network, from myth to reality

A few years ago, the network was a myth, and those who experimented with electronic means of communication were regarded as dreamy star-gazers. The network was a favourite topic of polite conversation: it was 'in' to talk about the existence and usefulness of it, and how long it would last, just as people used to do about the Internet. For many people, these 'new' methods were but costly fads, superfluous and snobbish, but while the talkers held learned conversations about whether the network idea was interesting or not, new companies were building their existence on it, and their growth. Netscape, for example, a household name today, developed and sold their browser using the resources of the Internet alone, with no distribution network, advertising or attractive packaging.

So, while the theorists were debating, the tools were being wheeled into position. Ten years ago, the facsimile was a novelty; today, people receive and send faxes over their mobile phones. Working in groups has become a reality thanks to electronic networks, and electronic data interchange (EDI) is a mere formality. Today, using processes once the preserve of the privileged few, millions of people from all over the world exchange data and work together in groups. At first there was only a trickle of traffic on the information highways; now, it is a crowded motorway. Video conferencing is in everyday use. The tools have taken us by surprise; we have been 'armed' without realizing it.

The cost of the network, the cost of transactions

The fact is that the cost of a classic Taylor organization is no longer competitive. When talking about the cost of an organization, we usually think of the direct costs associated with plant and personnel, to which a sum is added, of greater or lesser significance, for fixed expenses. However, an important, although often ignored, aspect of these expenses is the cost of transactions. As early as 1937,[2] Ronald H. Coase of the University of Chicago, who received the Nobel Prize for Economics in 1991, revealed the existence of transaction costs, showing that they arise from the choice made by the company: either to buy and subcontract externally or to produce internally. Buying on the market entails a transaction cost measured both in money and in time: arranging the price, setting up a contract, then following up and checking that it is carried out properly. On the other hand, internal production calls for other transaction costs: co-ordinating the flow of production, as well as recruiting, training, informing, and then forming the employees to fit the company. In other words, therefore, choosing to 'internalize' or 'externalize' production, to use the contemporary terminology, is a question of comparing internal and external transaction costs.

Formerly, the internal costs were more or less taken for granted: the challenge lay in finding and managing a variety of suppliers, and the market was neither as rich nor as well organized as it is today. Trying to enter faraway markets on one's own was an expensive folly. Today, subcontractors and those who place orders are to be found on the Internet. The costs of external transactions have been considerably reduced: it is common to appeal for tenders and make bids electronically, and software for drawing up documents or following up orders can even be downloaded free.[3] Getting in touch with a customer on the other side of the world is a simple matter today. For all these reasons, companies are externalizing and virtualizing many of their activities. Some transform themselves simply into centres of activity linked by the flow of information alone, thus reducing to a minimum all transaction and co-ordination costs.

As the classic pattern of organization is disappearing, the critics of the network begin to make themselves heard: 'OK, information circulates, but the decision-making process has been diluted.' 'It's total chaos, anyone can meddle in anything; there aren't any bosses any more, or rather there are too many bosses.' 'Look, the network is only this kind of matrix organization which all companies have tried at some point, and have later abandoned.' The men of marble, firmly entrenched in traditional patterns of organization, are still around: hypocritically, they extol the virtues of the open network, while maintaining control of the smallest details and upholding various non-productive barriers, all in the name of globalization, competition and the danger of industrial piracy and espionage. Others, less reticent, attempt to combine the actual structure of their organization with the network – but how can these two things be combined without losing one's footing in the process?

Even though the network may seem indispensable, few companies use it daily on a large scale. However, the stakes are enormous. The creation of added value is based on the exchange, at any place and at any time, of information and objects linked by a chain of value that spans the world. The thread that binds all this together is the intelligence of the group which controls, in space and time, the direction and the density of this chain value. Organizing the intelligent control of a network means getting hold of the tools provided within a given culture. Technology and culture – these are undoubtedly the two key factors here. So, the tools are available, but do we know how to use them? As far as the culture of the network is concerned, a thousand leagues removed from traditional hierarchical constructions, we do not possess it as yet, far from it.

How, then, are we to acquire and develop it? There are certain obstacles to be removed, certain gateways to be opened. There are four of them: two are ancient, two new; the former are technical in nature, and latter cultural. To open the first gateway, you have to learn trust; to open the second, you have to learn to use the new tools; and the third and fourth gateways cannot be opened until you have thoroughly assimilated and applied the new rules imposed by the *knowledge revolution*.

Trust is in

There is no need to break down the first gateway, as it is already open, at least in the realm of talk. The richness of the human capital available is positively celebrated, solemnly and vehemently propounded in professional discourse and company handouts. Book after book is published to promote trust, this new cornerstone of our societies, while at the same time the market for security and protection is flourishing as never before. People have never been more distrustful of their fellow men. The gap between theoretical discourse and reality is as wide as ever. Despite their denials, far too many company directors or government leaders still base their power on the retention of information, on veils of secrecy and the desire to prove that the skills and intelligence at their disposal surpass those of their rivals. This appears to be the price they are willing to pay to retain their power.

The future of wooden horses

Trust may be in vogue, but the adepts of the 'contract of mistrust'[4] are still going strong. One might have thought that they had disappeared, casualties of bankruptcy, mergers and the removal of production to other places, unable to resist the arrival of the new technologies that have shot the traditional company organization full of holes. Most of these people, docile products of the Taylor system, are to be found in the lower or middle echelons of the pyramid. The productivity of the new information tools has dealt them the death-blow: the routine work which they did has been automated; the data which they carefully sorted, organized and transmitted now travels without their aid via the company's information network. The men of marble at the base of the pyramid have disappeared – but what about those who live at the summit?

These people fall into three species, but only one species seems to have survived. The first species of men of marble has not survived. These are the 'frogs', who only know how to react in situations of extreme crisis, like a frog which, plunged into boiling water, makes a massive leap for freedom. Yet they have disappeared, just as frogs are boiled to death in a pan of cold water which is gradually brought to the boil. Without realizing it, they have been taken by surprise by gradual changes which have crept up on them – silent, but inexorable and irresistible. The second species were the 'elephants', somewhat clumsy creatures hopping from one foot to the other, alternately changing their organizations or personnel, never satisfied with the performance of either. Today, they are at the end of their tether; their great size, which was once a symbol of power and success, has now become a handicap. To assuage their fears they have changed their organization a thousand times, and their personnel even more frequently, but all to no avail. They have crumbled into dust. Bringing up the rear cavorted the 'wooden horses', the masters of the ring. They were trend-setters, astounding their competitors, but their calculating eyes were firmly fixed on the only point of reference that mattered – power. They still prance elegantly, ridden by those brilliant leaders who are always leading their companies into yet another devilish dance suggested to them by their dancing masters, the guru consultants: *re-engineering* in three-four time, TQM (total quality management) in four-four time, analyses of key competencies – dance upon dance *à la mode*, each one taken up with fresh vigour and then forgotten again as soon as the band begins to play a new tune.

Today's men of marble have taken refuge in the top of the pyramid. They are the carefully measured products of the management rationale that selected them, and using stock phrases culled from leading books on management they defend, in bad faith but with great acuity and agility, organizations that are often closed and blinkered, but which they deck out with sonorous names, abbreviations and slogans. There is often a yawning gap between the words they use and the reality of their companies: the base of the pyramid functions as a network, having often mastered the tools and acquired the necessary culture, whereas the summit seems to be stuck in the second industrial revolution. This is often evident in furnishings of another era, but can most clearly be seen in the fact that they themselves make little use of these new tools and the culture associated with them. In 1995, the French business magazine, *Entreprise*, carried out a survey of a representative section of top company managers. To their great surprise, the journalists discovered that most of them did not use a computer. Even worse, most of them seemed to find the very question ridiculous: 'Do I use a computer? You must be out of your mind! I employ people to do that!' The culture of the network is often foreign to them. They prefer the courteous and controlled formality of meetings held in an unpredictable mood of improvised conversations. While urging their employees to learn new skills, they themselves remain entrenched in the well-worn phrases of their prestigious degrees. Their positions are often well protected, free of any challenge from competitors if they hold senior management posts, and in no danger of being fired, since no one fires those whose job it is to fire others. In short, they extol the virtues of knowing how to delegate while holding their companies on a tight rein.

The return of old fears

Today, as in the past, one can recognize these people's companies by the fears that lurk there. The first of these fears, now as always, is the *fear of disorder*. Companies have become intangible. You can no longer comprehend them at a glance, and this fluid structure cannot be reduced to the cut-and-dried patterns of traditional company organization. Company directors accept that their personnel are dispersed geographically – as required by globalization – but some find the fact that they cannot be gathered together at any moment quite insupportable, and they are very tempted to centralize things again. Good excuses abound: what about a computer program that enables headquarters to link together all the company's databases; or how about organizing the company at the global level by types of job? In each case, behind these seemingly imperative and indisputable reasons, there lurk the fears of the management, who feel useless if they can no longer see the details of their company organization clearly. However, they will have to learn that it is no longer necessary to be able to 'see' a company organized as a network. Snapping your fingers no longer works; you have to learn how to click a mouse. Contacts are becoming more and more virtual, less and less physical. Many have tried to create theories to grasp this virtual disorder and make it scientifically respectable, by using laws of complexity, fractals, holograms and other natural principles of auto-organization. But is this really necessary? In daily life, company managers are well aware that their organization, that superb ship of the line, can founder in the next big wave. Running a business means constantly turning the ruling order into chaos; organization means trying to get the wanderers to march in the same direction. In order to describe this happy and fruitful cohabitation of order and chaos in a company, we might recall the term 'chaordic', coined by Dee Hock, the founder of the Visa credit card network.

The second *fear*, that *of losing power*, is more than ever present today. The classic pyramid with its ordered and stable levels is too costly today, and too unwieldy in the face of the nimble and agile newcomers. Spurred on by the fear of competition, from whichever quarter it may come, the wooden horses are constantly modifying the codes, slogans and landmarks with which they reassure themselves. They divide, cut back, slash out in all directions. Routine tasks have already been automated, computerized, and the middle echelons have disappeared. They play with words, concepts and new patterns of company organization, but the more they speak of transparency, the more opaque they become; the more they pepper their speech with the term 'empowerment', the more autocratic they become; the more they speak of trust, the more they distrust. Their fear of losing power prolongs their working hours;[5] rather than delegating or abandoning some of their power, they busy themselves even more, adding to their existing workload that of the middle echelons who have disappeared. They no longer have a minute to themselves, castigating and relentlessly controlling their own colleagues while they themselves are grossly overburdened. And so they find themselves in the position of the lamplighter in *Le Petit Prince* (The Little Prince): his planet revolves faster and faster, so that he no longer has the time to light and extinguish his single street lamp.

The third fear remains *the fear of new tools*. These tools of disorder, of subversion, have assumed such an importance that today it is impossible to ignore them completely, and so the men of marble have found a perfidious way of using them, which I shall return to later.

There is one final fear,6 rarely admitted and yet very common, and that is the fear of not being on top of things, of not making sufficient demands on oneself. This is the fear of becoming obsolete, of losing one's foothold, and it affects all of us, managers or employees, nourished by such factors as unemployment and job competition. Blinded by this fear, we are unable to see that the network, far from isolating us, is in fact a way of forging new links and of introducing us to new realms of knowledge, much more surely than classic patterns of organization, which lock us up in a world of hedged-in knowledge, bowling along the straight and narrow road that only permits the 'tried and true' to run at speed. The truth is that more than ever today all these additional fears form the breeding ground of distrust, and are its price.

The cost of distrust

Trust is in vogue because we all know that mistrust costs money. Returning to the ideas of R. H. Coase, the major cost of any transaction is that of bringing people together, and in order to reduce these costs any organization, be it a country or a company, has to reduce its level of distrust. Francis Fukuyama[7] quotes in this connection the example of Chinese or Italian families that seal their alliances with a simple gesture or even just a look, and which in this way have built up imposing industrial or commercial empires. At the opposite end of the scale, a society with a set of complex, nit-picking laws and all sorts of controls will be less efficient, since all collective action has to be based on rules duly committed to writing. The price of controlling all this is a whole distrustful arsenal of sophisticated checks and protective barriers. However, a society or a company based on these principles will in the end be more vulnerable, and will end up losing its foothold when faced with the mobility and supportive cohesion of its competitors. Distrust is costly when a company deploys and erects around itself walls, barriers, audits and a thousand other ways of controlling those people who make up the company and work for it.

The vicious circle into which distrust leads an organization is well known. It begins with something seemingly innocuous: an inexplicable order from on high which contradicts the common sense and experience of the man on the floor. It is pointless to disobey; heavy and brutal sanctions will soon serve to discourage even the boldest.

Gradually, people come to feel that they can no longer take the initiative, and in the end the desire to understand, to learn and to make progress disappears. What is the point of understanding when the only thing required for favourable recognition is to obey orders?

To conform, not to rock the boat, becomes the leitmotif of all, and the best way to shape a career. The blind promotion of the mediocre gradually lowers the quality of the company, which becomes impoverished and loses its competitive edge. At this point, the management begins to attribute the failure of their organization to the incompetence of their employees. Suspicion becomes entrenched, feeding a sense of mutual mistrust. The company is locked into its vicious circle. The management feels itself compelled to reinforce its apparatus of control and constraint, spewing out even more admonitions, rules and sanctions. At this point, distrust has come to stay, and so has the collective inefficiency of the organization.

In fact, of course, company directors who consciously build their organization on mistrust are rare. A few years ago, I explained this vicious circle of mistrust to the managers and employees of a certain European public organization. My presentation was followed by an icy silence, and then one of those present exclaimed: 'That's just what it's like here.' This comment was followed by a mixed chorus of rebuke and vociferous support. One of the senior managers, who was seated on the first row, rose and turned to address the gathering:

> Unfortunately, I am afraid that much of this analysis is true. We have inherited a set of constraining rules, the main purpose of which is to ensure the quality of our work, but which leave very little room for trust. We are all responsible for this state of affairs; it has become routine. By memo after memo and by adding to the rules and regulations, we have perfected the system without ever questioning it. Having said this, it seems to me that changing the rules would be difficult, because when it comes down to it trust is a state of mind and not something that can be decreed or laid down.

These lucid and telling remarks left us all speechless.

The price of trust

And what, indeed, would be the point of changing the rules, you might hear people ask? Those we have seem to work. All right, they tend to create distrust, but we cannot do much about that; this is the price to be paid for our efficiency. But is this always true?

Trust is in vogue because the efficiency of companies built on trust is a proven fact, but we hesitate perhaps to take the right steps because we are unsure of the new rules. Charles Handy lists seven of these.[8]

1. People say that trust is blind, but this is not true. People build trust with their eyes wide open; it is based on the vivid memory of a fruitful relationship or the mutual promise of shared success. In both cases it will only work if you know the people you are working with. As opposed to the classic type of organization, where people's functions and the rules that govern them preponderate, an organization set up as a network enables one to establish instant, ad hoc relationships with people who possess specific skills. A phone call, an e-mail suffice, and the contract of trust can be sealed just as surely as the mechanical relationships within classic hierarchies. The eyes of trust are wide open – it is distrust that is blind.

2. Distrust is blind and often knows no bounds, whereas trust establishes limits. Trust is built up around a precise task, and the results achieved will be evaluated later. The way in which they are attained is immaterial, whereas in an organization built on mistrust, the way tasks are carried out is scrupulously and punctiliously monitored, so much so that failure is often less castigated than non-observance of the rules.

3. Distrust is often an instinctive reflex. Trust, on the other hand, has to be learned. The trapeze artist launches himself into the air, and, all smiles, reaches out for his partner, who catches him in flight. The act has to be performed exactly right, every day, but every day conditions change. The mutual trust of the artistes is based on the repetition of certain actions. In a company, the efficiency of a team is based both on the ability of its members to perform well together today, and on their ability to renew their skills and their performance in the future.

4. Those who distrust accuse those who trust of being weak and soft-hearted, but if the truth be told, trust is without pity. Giving one's trust is not an act of weakness, and nor is withdrawing it. Since trust is the essential fuel which allows us to act more swiftly,

without the barriers, passwords and steel traps set up by mistrust, it is better to break off an agreement rather than reconstruct traditional barriers. The most efficient strategies of co-operation are those that self-destruct when one of the partners betrays the confidence of the other. This is the only way to make the offending party aware of what he risks losing by playing a double game.

5. Distrust creates distance, trust brings people together. A traditional company is held together by the solid cement of hierarchy, and of formalized rites and customs. The network just needs links, links that enable people to take concerted action even though the majority of the players are widely dispersed. The links take on various forms: they may be certain common values, or perhaps just a few simple words. In this way, for example, the 100,000 employees of Sodexho, spread throughout the world, are united around a few simple ideas: 'the team spirit, the service spirit, the spirit of progress'. These few words constitute a contract which can be referred to day by day.

6. Distrust dislikes face-to-face meetings, trust feeds on contacts. This is the only way in which to renew the contract that binds people together. In a network, each person acts autonomously. As there is an ever-present risk of being isolated, physical meetings are essential. Most frequently, nothing concrete emerges from such meetings except the reaffirmation of that *affectio societatis*, the desire to work together that is the basis of the juridical existence of an association. Meetings involve that wink of the eye or secret smile which confirm the pleasure of working together; seemingly harmless, often unperceived by others, these signs are the very heart of the contract of trust. A companion is someone with whom one breaks bread, and these meetings have symbolic value. They are also essential, since the memory of them will nourish the virtual meetings which will follow. This is why one may see cases in which complicated, risky contracts are entered into by a simple telephone call days, weeks or even years later. Such situations would be impossible without the reassuring memories supported by this trust constantly maintained and renewed.

7. Distrust calls for a few, distrustful bosses, whereas trust calls for trusting, interchangeable leaders. In fact, the principal criticism of the network idea is that there is no centre, no clear direction – in short, disorder. However, a network is not lacking in leaders. On

the contrary, each player is a leader in turn, or when his position calls for it. The desire to have just one leader reveals a lack of confidence in the others.

The culture of trust still has a long way to go. Moreover, it only reveals its efficiency in action. The point is that the techniques used must be favourable to trust; techniques and tools which are neutral in themselves can be turned in the right direction. In this way the second gateway may be opened and closed.

'Tool Story' – the insurgence of tools

This is a very enticing gateway to open. What could be more seductive, perhaps, than a fax with memory, a multimedia computer, a desktop scanner... all of these are tools, means and reasons for joining a network, for exchanging knowledge, for learning and for companies to work in a more flexible manner, less centralized and less localized. More and more, such tools are 'converging': your mobile phone receives written messages or faxes; it can link up to the Internet, and will soon be equipped with a video screen. Your television will become an Internet terminal, and the communication program in your laptop computer allows you to call the other side of the world at the cost of a local call. Your watch will no doubt become a digital camera for moving pictures or stills, and a screen for video conferencing. Whatever the device, it is becoming more and more communicative, interactive, multimedia.

Once the gateway has been opened, however, the daily reality may prove to be less futuristic: one finds that the tools are communicating, not the people. The rise in power of information hardware is impressive, but at the same time one has the impression that the more they are filled with technical refinements, the less they are pregnant with meaning. We end up as consumers of the tool rather than consumers of its usefulness. We accumulate, for example, watches, television sets, radios; channels of information multiply ad infinitum. The tools have become diverted from their purpose, and we surround ourselves with them more for their decorative value than their function. Thus, people have a mobile phone to show that they possess the 'sixth sense'[9] of belonging to a network, or a laptop computer to indicate that their time is precious.

On the other hand, these tools are more and more useful. They are our five senses, that of the cyberworld. Tools that capture, handle, store and transmit data, information and knowledge have become indispensable to us in terms of straddling the global market and advancing within the knowledge economy. Yet, as a chosen strategy or out of fatal ignorance, too many companies turn aside from their proper purpose the information tools at their disposal.

So it is that in many cases modern tools of communication are still assigned according to the status of those who use them rather than according to the use that could be made of them. Take, for example, a large public works company: those who supervise the work are on the road all the time, but are not equipped with mobile phones, whereas those at head office, who rarely leave the building, have been provided with them for a long time. So, no one can achieve personal gain from these advanced systems of information, but they are used to divide and separate people rather than unite them.

In fact, these new tools present such companies with insoluble problems. They are open systems, not easy to control, and therefore bring into question, in a technical yet very radical way, the styles of organization and the transmission of information within these companies. The network of links makes inroads into the hierarchy of power. Faced by such threats, companies reorganize to defend themselves against the new tools and their nefarious consequences. The first technique used here is to reserve the use of such tools to those who do not need them, as we saw in the above example concerning mobile phones. This is a well-tried strategy, which has been used since the introduction of company (or directors') cars.

The second technique consists in generously distributing such tools so that at all events they are democratically spread throughout the organization. Having done this, the next step is to render them virtually inoperative: passwords or sophisticated codes quickly deal a death blow to the information network, while answering devices and voice mailbox systems prevent direct communication.

The third technique aims at neutralizing the productivity of the tool by weighing it down with traditional procedures. Take for example the case of e-mails in one multinational company. The company is permanently linked by electronic post to its branches all over the world, but every morning the secretaries attached to the management dutifully print out all the messages received. In yet another 'modern' company, heads of department require copies of the e-mails sent to them by their colleagues to be placed in their in-tray.

There are other techniques which we will no doubt discover in the future if we keep our eyes open. The men of marble have incorporated mistrust and opacity of procedure into their management style. They often show more trust in their customers than in their own employees, and have erected around themselves a massive perimeter to protect them from prying eyes and keep others at a distance – a move which is quite acceptable because it authorizes indifference. In other words, for these people globalization has become an alibi for creating distance, and the network a way of dividing in order to rule.

Eggs and ideas

Mistrust may kill the network, and tools badly used may make it ineffective, but in fact the true obstacle is to be found elsewhere – the third gateway. In order to open it one has to acquire the essential reflexes of the economy of knowledge: a culture of information, the proper 'management' of intelligence, and above all a constant will to seek innovation.

Intelligence

Without the alliance of opposites or contrasting elements innovation is impossible, and yet innovation is only the result of a process driven by intelligence. What produces innovation, in fact, is the co-operative collaboration of different intelligences, but to activate these intelligences, the driving force, is an art not easily mastered. It is an art which has nothing in common with the art of setting material processes in motion, which inspired and drove on the industrial era. The management of intelligence (administration and organization) implies a different logic, a different style of organization.

In this case, the test is simple: is the intelligence of your company equal to the combined intelligences of those who work there? The IQ (intelligence quotient) of the company should be at least equivalent to the sum of the IQs of the employees. The question has to be asked even though it is impossible to answer. What point is there in collecting together the best brains, the best degrees and the most refined skills if the collective competence remains inadequate? What kind of alchemy creates or destroys this ephemeral assembly of skills that determines the genius or precipitates the fall of a company?

In the first place it is a question of *the collective management of time*. Time in terms of intelligence is not the same as time in terms of material things. Today, the time spent in occupations is less important than the time when we are preoccupied with thinking; physical presence is less important than mental presence. Those managers who are obsessed with rigid punctuality often learn to their cost that physical presence does not necessarily mean mental presence! François only works four days a week. He is a production engineer, but is also responsible for strategic investments. Each year he combs the lines of stands at the Hannover Trade Fair looking for those efficient machines that are the basis of the productivity and pride of his company. On the fifth day, François tends his beehives. He is an amateur beekeeper, and admits that he often selects the best machines while observing his bees patiently at work.

In the second place, it is a question of the *management of space*. The territory of intelligence is not limited as material things are. Two intelligences separated by thousands of kilometres can easily communicate; all that is needed is a good telephone line or an e-mail connection. In this way, Julien came to start his company almost by accident, on the basis of his passionate interest in the 'Pascaline', which is the name of the first modern calculating machine, invented by Blaise Pascal in 1640. There are only nine examples of this machine left in the world, most of them in museums.[10] Using an Internet search engine he made contact with other enthusiasts, an Australian and an Israeli, and within the space of a few hours they had exchanged plans and good ideas. This story is etched into Julien's memory, as this was the way he first met Jacob and Bob, who are now his partners in an international software company.

The third factor is the *management of the process of exchange*. Intelligence can neither be bought nor sold. It can be exchanged, pure and simple, but to do this calls for signs, words, a wink of the eye, smiles, active listening and dialogue. Intelligence is not fond of intermediaries that transform, or deform, its projects, but it is wild about meetings, challenges, questions. It needs recognition and attention. Having said this, however, intelligence is fragile. In order to work properly it needs sensors to collect it and then fuel to fire it. The collectors are our five senses: sight, hearing, touch, feeling and taste.

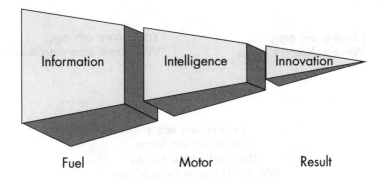

Fuel　　　　　　Motor　　　　　　Result

An intelligent company cannot allow itself to be deaf or dumb. It must see what is going on around it, both inside and outside. It must know how to use those modern tools that prolong our five senses: telephone, Internet, databases and video conferencing. Deprived of information, intelligence dries up.

Information

Information, the common contemporary currency, is the 'prime matter' of knowledge and the new fuel that drives the economy. Information is no longer just the shadow cast by objects. It can itself become a virtual object, and can even create new objects. DHL, for example, was established in 1969 to transport maritime documents by plane. These were the 'shadows' cast by the merchandise, and being able to do the paperwork before the arrival of the ships greatly accelerated customs procedures. Today, the merchandise itself is guided by information, although the companies that have mastered this new alchemic process are few and far between. Those who have, have become masters of information; having learned the essential rules of the exchange process, they have tamed information to suit their purposes.

Since innovation alone will enable us to 'sell what makes us different' in an increasingly competitive world, we now have to transmute the fuel of information into innovation by using the motor of intelligence. A new kind of know-how has to be mobilized. In the same way as one can buy and sell objects, we have to know how to buy and exchange information, but, in contrast to objects, the exchange of

I have an egg
We exchange eggs

You have an egg
We have one egg each

I have an idea
You have an idea
We exchange ideas
We each have two ideas

information has its own rules and its own economy. One does not exchange information as one would a mundane object.

The fact is that information becomes enriched as it is exchanged. 'I have an egg, you have an egg. If we exchange our eggs, we have one egg each. But if I have an idea, and you have an idea, and we exchange ideas, then we end up with two ideas each!' Through the simple fact of exchange, ideas become information from the point of view of the two people involved, and are transformed into knowledge. This is not an external object, but an internal enrichment. This may be a genuine Chinese proverb, or not, but using it within a company will support the circulation and exchange of information, and enrich the store of collective knowledge.

This is the last test: in your company, do you exchange information and ideas like you would exchange eggs or other mundane objects? Do you use the tit-for-tat logic of barter or that of mutual enrichment? To give a proper reply to this question we have to totally revise our understanding of information. Information can either be a simple datum or a sacral image. For many of us it is the modest shadow cast by objects, but not in itself an object of exchange.

Sacral image?

It took thousands of years for pictograms to evolve into writing, but in the course of a few decades digitalization has shattered the old representation of the world and reconstructed a new reality. Images move, and multiply incessantly; sound became music and can now be reproduced at will. Soon, taste, smell and touch will be digitalized, but we are already confused by the forms digitalization takes today. Our five senses are faced with new temptations in this virtual world, but we have to flush out the real hiding behind the virtual, and vice versa. Information flits here and there, feather-light, but it makes us afraid. At the root of most religions there is often a book, a myth, a written or oral tradition, and in this sense information is still a sacral image. There is some information it would be sacrilege to publish, like the incunabula consigned to 'hell' in medieval libraries. They are jealously guarded and only unveiled on very special occasions, like the Black Virgins of Holy Week in Andalusia. Whether essential or of minor importance, information hides away, caught somewhere between modesty and shame on the one hand, and avarice and greed for gain on the other.

Today, however, the times are rapidly changing. The sharp glare of the media shines into every crevice. Censorship has become very difficult; those who surf the Internet sail on oceans of codified information. In a few years' time, the vast majority of books in print, from the Bible to the most recent publications, will be digitalized and accessible through keywords. 'If it is not digitalized, our culture will disappear', predicts Alain Minc.[11]

> This massive digitalization poses a major problem of cultural identity. The foundations of a society are its memory and its language... digitalization alters the relationship to knowledge. When children surf the Internet, from one data base to another, digitalized knowledge replaces book knowledge, and in this way their attitude to knowing is totally changed.

This is what is happening to texts from Ancient Greece: the Perseus Project, involving universities throughout the world, has set itself the task of digitalizing all the classical authors. Choose a word, and all the uses of it will immediately appear, from Xenon to Aristophanes via Plato, Thucydides and Herodotus. It is also a fact that a large part of the documentation required for this present book was taken directly from databases available on the Internet: magazine articles in *Fortune* and *Forbes*, or from *Business Week*, *L'Expansion*, *Libération*, *Le Monde* and *Courrier International*. These enquiries were conducted using keywords. There are so many easily accessible sources, often free. The Internet network is a metaphor for the knowledge network: everything is available, but only to those who seek. Even when digitalized, the contours of information are often unclear, and the boundaries between data, information and knowledge are often fluid. If you ignore these differences, you can destroy information and knowledge, leaving only raw data, which is useless.

Data or knowledge?

A piece of data is, for example, a measure of temperature (30 °C) or of air pressure (1,010 millibars). Data becomes information when it finds a context: '30 °C, that's warm for this time of year.' The knowledge which follows from this is, perhaps, 'Let's go to the beach. This good weather can't last.' The difference between data, information and knowledge is due to the intervention of man, who perfects in this way his knowledge of things, and his representation and interpretation of reality. A piece of data is by definition accessible, but it is up to us to see it and capture it, since a human brain is needed to transform it into knowledge. Making it accessible means understanding, and making others understand, that it is only fuel for the motor of intelligence.

Another reason why information is fragile is that it can evaporate when distributed. It only remains alive and fresh when you pluck it yourself. Some feel that distributing it means deciding in advance the use to which it is to be put. Others believe that knowledge can be put on like a garment off the shelf, whereas in fact it is a very personal thing. For all these reasons, and many others, information is often badly treated.

The obstacles

Acquiring a culture of information means first and foremost identifying and ruthlessly eliminating the obstacles which prevent us from exchanging it. The pitfalls connected with this process are well known.

The most common one is the closed-door syndrome. It involves the deliberate hiding of information. Our natural curiosity, which tends to leave doors open, is aroused when it runs into closed doors behind which information is hidden from us. 'What's in there?', we ask, 'A broom cupboard or Bluebeard's den?' Within a company, doors are sometimes permanently closed, either by negligence or design, but a closed door gives birth to rumours and raises ghosts: 'If this information is being kept locked away, it must be really worth something!' How are we to open doors inadvertently closed? By using all the means of dialogue at our disposal – works committees, meetings – to answer all the questions that might be asked, no matter how silly or taboo they may be. Now this exercise might appear dangerous, but experience shows that information quickly given more quickly kills a rumour than any number of attempts at justification later on. 'There's no smoke without fire', as the old saying goes. So why let smoke envelop the company if there is no fire?

The second pitfall is more elusive. Those who fall into it are companies which, in order to avoid the dangerous closed-door position, decide to set up a procedure for the distribution and sharing of information. The channels of information are formalized, labelled, institutionalized, but unfortunately, because the information that can be accessed and distributed is carefully selected, this procedure dries up or blocks the ordinary flow of daily information vital to the life of the company. The package, which is impeccably designed and both logically and strategically correct, suppresses the information culled at ground level, which is uneven and unpredictable in form. When the fuel handed out is of a foreseeable kind, it becomes less potent. If intelligence dries up and has only pre-digested information to work on, how can one innovate? Information theorists will tell you that the value of information lies precisely in its singularity; the more it is foreseeable, the less its value. In order to provide a rich fuel, it is necessary to mix ritual procedures and improvised happenings, to mingle glossy handouts with doodles on the backs of envelopes. In order to work properly, intelligence needs surprises.

The daily workings of a company have to be nourished in the light of the following three simple observations. The question is: how? How are we to treat information without maltreating it? How to make use of the intelligences around us? How to ensure that these intelligences meet each other in order to innovate rather than merely reproduce, or worse, self-destruct?

Innovation

Innovation is the source and the effect of change, and it is here we have to begin. More surely than ever before, the harnessing of space and time and the profusion of contacts lead to that 'improbable encounter' that generates innovation, a chance encounter of ideas and minds that comes as a shock both to objects and situations. From this point onwards, innovation steals a march on mere reproduction. Acquiring this reflex, central to the network, means knowing how to man the lookout posts, managing, like an impresario or an actor, the rare exchange of information or ideas which had no logical reason to meet. The fact is that we know how to meet people familiar to us, but feel clumsy in the face of strangers. Innovation means creating alliances between differences, even opposites. Innovation means knowing how to create these alliances, and in order to acquire this reflex one has to pass a basic test!

The following story is authentic, and concerns the board of a large industrial concern. Globalization was on the agenda, in the shape of a proposed alliance with another concern, an old rival. The discussion was lively, the various points of view crossed swords. Finally, the president of the board suggested that, as a strategic necessity, time should be taken to study the proposed alliance in more detail. At this point, one of the members of the board took the floor and suggested that a short test should be carried out to try the ability of the concern to enter into an alliance. He turned to his neighbour and placed his elbow on the table with his arm bent and his palm open upwards, as if preparing for a bout of arm-wrestling. 'This is the game', he explained, 'the winner, or winners, are those who can touch the shoulder of their partners the greatest number of times.' Somewhat surprised, the members of the board began the exercise, unwillingly at first, then with enthusiasm. They flexed their muscles, but the encounters remained friendly. After a while, the contestants turned to face their instructor. Casting a disapproving eye on the winners, who were puffing with the exertion, he announced that the real winners were two board members who, instead of striving against each other, had without effort and with considerable enjoyment used the solid pivot of their locked elbows to make rapid to-and-fro movements from the shoulder of one to the shoulder of the other. The same rules applied to all, but most of the contestants had chosen to interpret them as a struggle between two people, with a victor and a loser. Few had seen the possibility of an alliance and shared victory. The rules of the game allowed for both positions: 'The winner, or winners, are those who can touch the shoulder of their partners the greatest number of times. These are the victors.' Those who had chosen to form an alliance had combined their strengths and had won without effort.

Many leaders of companies have done this test, and in the majority of cases the contestants choose confrontation. On each occasion, however, there are a few who move their forearms in unison from one shoulder to the other. The possibility of co-operating without changing the rules of the game always seems to come as a surprise.

The levers that move the network

The last gateway opens. Trust has reduced the cost of transactions, the tools are being efficiently used. The culture of information infuses the whole company, intelligences are co-operating. Now it is time to organize the network around a set of simple rules.

Utility, the culture of 'why?'

Here is the first fundamental rule: a company is primarily a product which the market finds useful, and the members of a network must be able to recognize and share the usefulness of the company to which they belong. This ought to be true of all organizations. However, there are some organizations which seem to spend most of their energy on simply surviving the disappearance of their original usefulness. If they looked around them they would see that history has made a permanent inventory of institutions that have passed away, from the drivers of horse-drawn carriages to those who made sails for schooners. To defend and preserve the beauty and nobility of a trade that has lost its usefulness is indeed a very dangerous temptation. As we explained in some detail above, a trade is not the property of those who exercise it: if there are no customers, then the trade is a mere pastime, a historical curiosity.

A company becomes a network when its financial and social utility is shared by all its members, and has become their daily obsession – when the culture of 'how?' has been replaced by the culture of 'why?'

The culture of 'how?' is the docile culture of the Taylor style of institution which has thoroughly codified procedures: following the instructions was a guarantee of efficiency. The culture of 'how?' is a culture that conforms to predetermined processes, but today many of these processes are fully automated. Faced by permanent change, the key to an organization's success lies in its ability to be reactive, its capacity to analyse an ongoing situation. Of course, it is necessary to act and to find an efficient mode of action, but before this one has to understand why things have suddenly changed. Analysing the root causes of the reality one is faced with enables one to discern and plot out the possible directions in which things might move.

Some people might raise their eyebrows on reading these lines. What happens to established procedures? How can our company become ISO certificated? This is precisely the point. It is easier to explain and apply a procedure when you know its *raison d'être*, than to apply fixed procedures, the usefulness of which is obscure.

The question 'why?' is not subversive. It is a question of ends and aims. Accepting this culture means that company managers agree to answer all the questions put to them, no matter how stupid or indiscreet they might be. This is by no means a waste of time, but a recognition of the importance of human intelligences to the process of building up a company. If you spend time discussing the ends, those essential 'why?' questions, then you will be able more quickly to move on to the 'how?' questions concerning means.

Identity, recognition

The second fundamental rule of a network is the recognition of the identity of its members – knowing people and making oneself known makes for a better exchange at all levels. A classic style of organization is not interested in people's identity; it is only interested in functions, status. What you say is of little importance; what counts is the position you are speaking from and the function that you represent. Several years ago, for example, I took part for the first time in one of these exercises which are typically French: the preparation of 'the Plan'. When I arrived at the place where the meeting was to be held, a large, panelled room, a few people were already waiting, seated at the other end of the room. I sat down next to them, and gradually the room filled up. The chairman of the board, who later became a famous government minister, opened the meeting. The discussion became animated. I took the floor and expounded a particular idea. To my great surprise, the leader of the employer's delegation rose to face me with magisterial anger and tore my arguments to shreds. At that point I realized that I was seated among the trade union delegates, disguised, no doubt, by their ties. Thinking I belonged to the enemy camp, the manager who stood up to face me had not paid attention to what I said, but to the place from which I said it. In traditional organizations, you are identified by your status or your title, and for this reason your contribution has to be finely adjusted, and should not cause surprise. There are other meetings where you have to wait until the end to find out who the participants were; you have to take people aside and ask who it was who expressed this or that point of view. When the meeting is over, the problems at hand have not been tackled, but everyone is delighted to have finally discovered 'who is who'.

In a network, functions are not primary; only relationships matter and the content which they bear. The speed with which a process can be mobilized is the essential factor. The vital point is to know to whom you should pass the baton, no matter what their official function or status. The important thing is what they can do for you now, in the given situation.

The rules surrounding identity are simple. Never start a meeting without making sure that all those present know each other. In the same way, do not hesitate when introducing a new topic to check the level of knowledge of those present. Too many leaders seem to forget that life does not stop when people leave the company buildings; their employees read, listen to the radio, have opinions, passionate interests and fields of erudition in which they are experts. To ignore this is to deprive the company of some vital trump cards.

The rapid spread of the Internet allows for personal identities to be brought out and exchanged. Employees can each be given a welcome page where they can present themselves, the projects on which they are working and the specific skills that they possess. In this way, British Petroleum has arranged for the creation of tens of thousands of personal web pages. Not only does this allow those wishing to exchange information to get to know their interlocutor better, it also makes it possible to search out the person whose centre of interest and list of contacts are best suited to one's purpose. A simple search engine, supplied with the keywords which you have chosen, will be able to select for you, out of the thousands of keywords in the network, the skills and individuals which you need to further your work or your project.

Interactivity, relationships

The efficacy of a network, therefore, is built up around the density and frequency of relationships. Like the human brain, the quality of a network does not depend on its size, but on the number of connections that the 'neurons' of the network can establish between them; the interactivity of each 'neuron', of each member of the network, is measured by the number of 'dendrites' radiating out from each of them.

In a traditional company that exchanges 'objects', interactivity is a waste of energy. Dialogue is pointless, as each person knows his place, his role. On the other hand, interactivity is a source of enrichment when it is a question of the exchange of ideas – information is enriched when it is exchanged! To receive and give, to give in order to receive, this is the new breathing pattern of the company. Its efficiency is measured by the ability of its members to exchange information all the time, without barriers or administrative routines.

Malcolm Dow of Northwestern University, well known for his work on the analysis of networks, tells the following illuminating story in this connection. The president of a large American consortium hired a financial director. After a few months, the president became uneasy; it seemed to him that the new member of his team was not fitting in properly. Malcolm Dow then found out that the financial director, who was younger than the company president, had quite a different way of communicating: thoroughly at home with the telephone and the e-mail, he had built up his network in the course of a few months. The leaders of the organization seemed to have accepted him very well, but the links he had established were invisible to the company president, who totally relied on meetings and other forms of physical contact. The point is, though, that interactivity is not measured by the number or length of meetings, but by the ability to straddle space and time, whether virtual or physical.

Simplicity, the exchange of basics

Simplicity is the fourth lever. Globalization has created gigantic companies, the largest of which can only just keep track of the people they employ. How can such companies be expected to make sure that the hundreds of thousands of people who are supposed to work together can in fact communicate satisfactorily? The tools available today allow for direct contacts, without intermediaries. A single gesture is enough to establish such a contact, at almost no cost. The problem is that traditional organizations were formed at a time when it was difficult to imagine that one could communicate from one end of the world to the other for the price of an ordinary local call.

Simplicity also requires that there are no intermediaries between those involved. Whether intermediaries are required or not is up to the members of the network themselves to decide; links cannot be decreed, they simply arise as needed. Simplicity disappears, however, when sophisticated systems of communication, such as steering or evaluation committees, end up by absorbing most of the energy resources of a network, so that those involved in the network no longer have the time to manage their contacts.

Finally, simplicity requires one to concentrate on aims and gradually formulate the rules as required. True networks establish a minimum set of rules which guarantee that the objective is reached without delay. Like the typical disorder of artists' studios or writers' studies, networks love the relaxed and unforeseeable disorder of the flow of information, while abhorring the immediate, ordered, clinical cleanliness of planned structures, however well intentioned.

As the first really globalized units, companies are confronting the new challenges of the market, of knowledge and of the networks, but they are not alone: individuals, nations, whole societies are taking the quantum leap along with them. The project has taken on a collective character, but it is all the more difficult and dangerous for all that.

Notes

1. François Lenglet, '2007, la vie quotidienne au temps de la néo-économie', *L'Expansion*, No. 546, 3–16 April 1997.
2. *The Nature of the Firm*, New York, O. E. Williamson and S. G. Winter, 1937.
3. Programs from PeopleSoft can be paid for over the Internet.
4. Cf. *La Porte du changement s'ouvre de l'intérieur,* Paris, Calmann-Lévy, 1992.
5. 'Le Temps de travail des cadres', *Le Monde*, 10 October 1996.
6. Thanks to Jean-Marie Descarpentries for drawing my attention to this fourth fear, which is obvious and yet secret.
7. Francis Fukuyama, *Trust*, New York, Free Press, 1995.
8. Charles Handy, 'Trust and the Virtual Organization', *Harvard Business Review*, May–June 1995, p. 40.
9. Advertisement for SFR, 1997.
10. 4 in Paris (CNAM), 2 in Clermont-Ferrand (musée du Ranquet), 1 in Dresden (Staatlicher Mathematisch Salon), 1 in the private collection of Léon Parcé, 1 in the IBM collection.
11. *Le Monde Informatique*, 14 July 1995.

4 Citizens or Visitors?

THE COMPANY AND SOCIETY

Kai-sha, the company
Sha-kai, society

Inside, a cool, golden light suffused the walls; outside, the maize was bone-dry in the August sun. The village church was full to bursting point. Never had so many people turned up for the burial of a *harki* (French soldier from the colonies – tr. note). On this his last day, it was not the nation for which he had fought that was paying him the last honours, but the company for which he had worked for more than 25 years. Here, in the middle of the summer, almost all of his colleagues had gathered, not called together by any company memorandum, but simply by the memory of his laugh. On that day more than any other I was proud of my company.

All of us can remember such moments of solidarity, when a company assumes the reassuring face of a family, of a nation, or perhaps the familiar landscape of one's childhood. On the other hand, how many mining towns have not been lulled into unsuspecting sleep in the shadow of long-established, large local companies, which have suddenly bowed under? How many regions have not lost their industrial pride when the blast furnaces were shut down? How many countries have not lost their dominant position when competitors have invaded their ports?

Perhaps companies should simply be cold-hearted capitalist nomads, relinquishing to the State, as the sole guarantee of caring, justice and stability, the task of checking and balancing their versatility and irresponsibility?

This is a cul-de-sac discussion, the preserve of schizophrenic politicians and company managers filled with unrighteous indignation. The answer is to be found elsewhere, in the process of exchange. A company is formed from what it gives and what it receives. The millennium which has now reached its close has seen the birth and development of human exchanges of all kinds, widening out from the city to embrace the whole world. Slowly and inexorably, the market has grown. In this incessant to-and-fro process not only have products and services been exchanged, but also epidemics, cultures, emotions and convictions, religions, ideas, solidarity, democracy... in a word, life in all its aspects.

Human exchange is the lifeblood of the individual, of society and of nature. Companies, which are one of the driving forces behind such exchanges, are nourished by and nourish these three spheres. Without each of these parties and the exchanges that take place between them there would be neither life nor wealth. It is perhaps the unique responsibility of companies to link and preserve these three spheres.

There is a symmetry between the company and society; they are complementary to each other, as are the words for them in spoken and written Japanese. The company (*kai-sha*) becomes society (*sha-kai*) by reversing the ideograms that represent these two concepts.[1] France was late discovering this fruitful symmetry, and regularly forgets about it, although it is omnipresent: the opening out of France to Europe and of Europe to the world has made the company an essential locus for the creation of wealth which is demonstrable and indispensable. At the same time, the entry of women into the workforce and increasing urbanization have turned companies into social units with a special role and status.

Today, however, the siting of companies within the social landscape has changed. Having become globalized, they are no longer enclosed within the nation, as they were formerly. The game they are involved in, the issues at stake, reach far beyond their own back garden and the local community. Companies are straddling the gulf between two seemingly irreconcilable objectives. On the one hand, they are becoming globalized, entering the virtual world in order to improve their products and spread them more widely, making use of the most productive people and resources. While on the other hand, in order to match the competition, they have to ensure delivery on the ground to customers who are anything but virtual, served by employees of flesh and blood. Society, for its part, offers a haven to companies which are less and less national, either totally or partially global. Society would like these companies to have 'citizenship', whereas many of them are already quite satisfied with a 'visitor's permit'.

The global chain of value which companies live off questions the very foundations of many countries. Some discover that they are no longer perforce the exclusive preserve of the creation and distribution of wealth; companies are always looking for places where the grass is greener. Others become aware that the global perspective reduces their importance as an individual country. In a sense, all nations discover that they are at the same time both too small and too large in the face of these new conditions. Too small: more and more countries are forming alliances (NAFTA, AELE, ASEAN) designed to tie down these roving chains of global value, offering them both a place to settle and the skills needed for production, as well as an avid consumer market. Too big: a large interior market, like in the 19th century, is no longer an assured source of wealth if trading totally disregards frontiers. This is doubtless the reason why small countries, such as Singapore and Denmark, feel that their national growth and their companies are at ease on the global market. On the other hand, nations as a concept are not dead, they simply have to find new spheres of legitimate action, such as: the regulation of markets, and of competition; the redistribution of produced wealth (rather than the a priori pre-emption of productivity gains through income taxes); the protection and development of individuals over and above purely financial considerations. These are the stakes of the future game – as yet often poorly defined, sometimes even hardly perceived – and the cause of future leaps into the unknown.

Society's quantum leap

'Societies flourish when beliefs and technology are congruent.'[2] Today, this convergence does not seem to be working. In the short term, technology, totally oriented towards the search for productivity, leads to a reduction in the amount of work available. While society, grown confident by decades of prosperity, has placed work at the centre of things, because work is at one and the same time a source of revenue, of status and social position, of prosperity and the redistribution of wealth.

On the other hand, the more work supports the redistribution of wealth, the greater are the costs associated with it, and as a result economic planners have less and less recourse to it; in France, as in the rest of Europe, the social services constantly raise the price of work. Today, those who safeguard the common weal have many responsibilities: to protect the health and income of the elderly, of those in early retirement, of the middle-aged; to ensure the insertion of young people into the job market, the education of youth, and so on.

The task facing them has become even more difficult because, for the first time in history, four generations are living side by side: from the 3-year-old great-grandchild to its 80-year-old great-grandfather, three generations are growing up, studying, or enjoying their leisure, while only one generation is actually working. Three generations are beginning to squabble over the distribution of the wealth produced by the fourth. In France, between 1980 and 1995, the incomes of those at work rose by 0.4% per annum, while those of retired people rose by 4% per annum.[3] In the year 2030, people aged 65 and over will represent 40% of the active population, as opposed to 20% in the year 2000 and 19% in 1960. In Germany, this figure will be approaching 50%![4] Consumers buy at the most favourable price, without worrying too much about the social imbalance their purchases might entail. Thus society redistributes wealth as well as it can, and as cheaply as possible.

Companies, for their part, adapt, move to other locations, or maintain their position. As passive citizens, companies in France hand over to society for redistribution half of the wealth that they produce, but as active citizens, companies should be aware of the use they make of the resources entrusted to them by society. The market for economic resources has been regulated for a long time now, and international summit meetings supplemented by local legislation have gradually built up systems to control ecological resources. But what about the human resources? Companies make use of, maintain and renew the intelligence of the people they employ, but they do not develop this intelligence in the first place. Indeed it would seem that today, whether by negligence or inertia, developed societies tend to select rather than foster, to maintain rather than develop, the intelligence of their citizens. In 1993, UBS, the Union of Swiss Banks[5] carried out a study to measure the 'growth curve' of various countries. The study produced both an index of the growth of investments in technology and human resources and an index of efficiency in these areas. The results showed that Asian countries were ahead both in terms of human and technical resources, while the developed countries, such as

France, were behind, apparently gripped by inertia in terms of promoting development through the education of intelligence.

The crisis of nations or of society reveals another crisis, that of the mode of government. In France, the forces of Jacobinism and rhetoric, which achieved miracles in the past in terms of constructing and cementing the identity of France as a nation and as a society, have now lost their power to remove uncertainty and mobilize a common effort. While changes are daily taking place all around us – through dialogue, learning and experimentation – we continue to revise a corpus of complex laws full of high intentions, implemented by statutes that completely ignore the justice or relevance of the original intentions behind the laws. We sincerely applaud the spontaneous civic responsibility shown by our fellow citizens in difficult moments, in connection with strikes or solidarity movements, but at the same time we continue to govern them as subjects. What applies to a company applies equally to society: in a complex system, rules are important, but even more important is the way they are observed. The secret of success or failure lies not in the minute observance of rigid rules, but in the behaviour of the people involved, the way they see things, and the way they act and learn together.

It seems we have not meditated enough on these words of Peter Drucker: 'The key to the creation of riches will not be either the allocation of capital for production purposes, or work – these two poles of economic theory in the 19th and 20th centuries, be it classic, Marxist, Keynesian or neo-classic. Nowadays, value is created by productivity and innovation, which are both applications of knowledge to work.'[6]

Work quantum leap

'There is no lack of work. It is we who lack the clear-sightedness to understand that work is changing radically, and the imagination to organize it in a different way. In twenty years' time, no matter what we have done or not done, there will still be several million people out of work in France or the French will be working in a different way.'[7]

The quantum leap in the world of work began two centuries ago. Wage-earners were a rare species at that time, mostly employed in agriculture. At the outset of the industrial revolution, wage-earners lived at home or with their employers. At the beginning of the 19th century, the first factories were built in an effort to increase efficiency and productivity. Wages, which had previously depended on custom or some judicial decision, were now fixed by the rules of competition. At the beginning of the 20th century, mass production and Taylor-inspired industrial organization launched the industrial society. Protection of wage-earners gradually improved – provisions concerning accidents at work, social security, retirement schemes, and so on – but wages did not follow gains in productivity. Wages were a cost to be minimized. The demand for industrial benefits did not follow the increasing power of production. This was one of the causes of the crisis of 1929.

After the Second World War, things changed. Under the influence of the economic theories of John M. Keynes and the social visions of William H. Beveridge, the State became 'The Welfare State', and governments developed policies to stimulate demand, favour full employment and allow wages to more or less follow gains in productivity. In France, the guaranteed minimum wage (SMIC) became a reality on 11 February 1950. The post-war growth years marked the apogee of the wage system. The crisis of 1973 swung the pendulum back the other way. In retrospect, one can see that wages had grown faster than the productivity rate. At the beginning of the 1970s, wages rose more than 8% per annum, one point above the rise in productivity. Ten years later, the balloon burst: wages were growing at 15%, while productivity had reached a ceiling at less than 4%.[8] Wages refused to fall, unemployment increased. In effect, work had become a rare and cherished product, and state intervention was increasingly indicated: non-intervention, privatization and a flexible job market became the slogans of many politicians. Employment contracts of indefinite duration are becoming the exception (70% of the new contracts signed in 1996 were contracts with a fixed duration).

As I am writing these lines, unemployment is still on the high side. The unemployed have begun to organize themselves and even take to the streets, while the most brilliant minds expatiate on the subject in reports, offer solutions and propose legislation, sometimes simple, sometimes extremely complicated. European governments meet regularly to share their experiences in this matter. The introduction of the Euro has enabled them to measure public deficits almost to the decimal point, but they seem unable to agree on a common level for the rate of unemployment. One fiscal fashion succeeds the other: tax relief, a reduction in working hours, subsidized employment. Each season brings its fresh crop of comparisons: 'The USA is creating more jobs', say some, while others retort that it is creating even more poverty. The cynics explain that an increase in poverty is normal in countries with a weak system of social redistribution, while it is unpardonable for us to have so many marginalized people when half of our wealth is redistributed. Each year a new country is brought forward as a paradigm of virtue: The Netherlands is cited as an example, or Denmark, quite forgetting in the process that earlier it was in vogue to praise the successes of Germany, lambaste Great Britain, make fun of Italy and ignore Portugal. The whole thing ended up like the squabbling doctors in Molière's play. Having been bled again and again, 'le Malade Imaginaire' is in pretty bad shape today.

The three ages of work[9]

Our present conception of work is inherited from Adam Smith. In the society in which he lived, each person had his or her position and place. Companies made sure that their labourers received a just wage, that the chain of command was respected and that competition was strangled at birth. However, his 'invention' of the division of labour caused a breach in this stable structure. 'In each species', he wrote, 'the division of labour, carried to the furthest extent possible, yields a proportional increase in the productive power of work.'[10] Applying this thesis, Smith adduced his famous example of the manufacture of pins: if the production of a pin is broken down into 18 separate steps, with workers specializing in each of them, the same amount of work will multiply production by a factor of nearly 5000. The division of labour, a child of the industrial revolution, has led to the measurement of the quantity of work contained in goods exchanged by various specialized manufacturers. Work has become an abstract quantity, a product of the exchange of goods. In consequence, industrialized societies have confused work with paid work. Today, after 50 years of the Welfare State, in everyday language the term 'work' is used without differentiation to designate 'work', 'activity', 'income' and 'job'. It is vitally important that we remove this confusion.

One can distinguish between three 'ages' of work which today are hopelessly confused.

First of all, work is *production*. Along with capital and land it is one of the three factors in production listed by Adam Smith. This function of work is not in question; the aim of work will always be to create wealth. On the other hand, wealth is increasingly immaterial: 'In twenty years' time, the percentage of Frenchmen directly employed in the manual transformation of material things (workers, farmers) will be considerably less than 20% of the active population (who remembers that at the end of the 1930s some 60% of wage-earners were workers?).'[11] The consequences of this evolution are opening up before our eyes. Trades are evolving and end up by resembling each other. Increasingly, we are sitting in front of a computer screen, reading, interpreting or adding information. Work is becoming less material, and this alters the skills called for to carry out the new trades. Reproduction of a purely repetitive type is the domain of robots and automated systems, whereas work has become an act of permanent creation. This applies, for example, to a computer programmer, but also to the company employee who has to cope with the unforeseeable requirements of customers, and to the system operator who has to identify and remedy sudden computer crashes. Work is also a question of relationships. The employee who formerly sat in splendid isolation in front of his machine is today a member of a team that is both actual and virtual; he is in direct touch with his customer, his supplier and his partners. Last, work has become a lifelong learning process. One's store of applied knowledge quickly becomes obsolete, and new knowledge has constantly to be acquired. Productive learning is a discipline required of us every day.

Second, work is *a tool of emancipation*. The political and economic revolutions of the 18th century individualized work. In France, the principle of equality contributed to the suppression of the guilds in 1791, and opened the way to a new contract, the 'contract of hire', which was made official in 1804: 'A contract of hire which is not limited in duration can at any time be revoked at the will of one or other of the contracting parties.'[12] Yet there is a reverse side to liberty: emancipation and alienation were to become the two contradictory aspects of this evolution. Alienation was denounced by Karl Marx and by Louis René Villermé, a former surgeon in Napoleon's army who violently opposed the exploitation of children, who were put to work for something like 12 hours a day from the age of 8. Progressive emancipation, achieved through the social conflicts of the 19th century, re-established the balance of relationships between employers and employees.

In the third place, work is a *means of social stratification*. The 40-hour week, paid holidays and the consumer society have contributed to the development of the middle classes, which today are the essential pillars of society. The contract of employment has gradually become a social statute, so much so that today 80% of the active French population are wage-earners. Through the medium of work, women have achieved a status which previous societies had denied them:

> In the course of thirty years, since the beginning of the 1960s, the active male population has only increased by one million, whereas the active female population has grown by 4.5 million; to be exact, it grew by 3 million in the period from 1975 to 1990, which is the period in which unemployment exploded in France.[13] In the course of this process, the direct, individual remuneration for work done has decreased in favour of a redistribution of wealth in the form of social benefits either general (health services, family allowances, unemployment benefits) or specific (pensions).

Towards a contract of activity

Work is creative, relational, formative and less material. It has apparently preserved all the qualities it possessed at its origins two centuries ago, so what is the cause of the present crisis? Work, which is the only corridor to life in a modern society, is a source of wealth, but also of injustice: being simply a citizen often confers fewer social rights and political influence than being a wage-earner. At the same time, wide gaps are opening up between various groups: between those who are in work and the unemployed; between those in stable employment in large companies and those in unstable companies whose positions are more insecure; between those who work with knowledge, at ease within the space of the electronic market, and those who have nothing else to offer but their time and the somewhat futile strength of their arms.

Some people see in this situation the effects of the end of the ideological competition between communism and capitalism. In order to match the statistics and triumphant images of the other camp, our capitalist societies were forced to offer proof of progressive social measures. Once the competition was removed, this 'social programme' came to a halt.[14] Others[15] regard work and the fulfilment it offers as the last manifestation of Pascal's 'diversion', a ridiculous strategy to help us forget the approach of death. However, these views, no doubt pertinent in themselves, do not take account of a more particular crisis. The functions of work – production, emancipation and social stratification – will doubtless constitute the basis of our society for a long time to come. The problem is the type of work done by wage-earners today, which was well adapted to the concentrated efforts called for by industrial mass production, but no longer meets the need for a flexible response to changing and exacting customer demands.

In fact the status of work has changed. Formerly, the contract of hire was set within a collective framework. The security of full employment, although implicit, was a tangible social benefit, almost to the point of being a right; a career plan coupled with on-the-job training marked out a secure future. Today, however, the contract of hire is based on individual responsibility.

Security[16] has disappeared, to be replaced by insecurity. The old trades, although not yet dead, are already obsolete, while new trades are cutting their teeth. The knowledge economy is gradually replacing the traditional industrial economy. Meanwhile, as we do our best to get up to a new cruising speed, we suffer the tribulations of adaptation to new conditions. Will we have to wait for long? No one really knows.

In the past, work was an assured means of promotion; today, each person has to promote his own career. The company is no longer the tutelary god of former times. Indeed, companies are beginning to question their own long-term survival, and can no longer guarantee a career plan, or at least only a zigzag plan involving changing jobs in the company several times. No guarantees, however – the perimeter of the company can change at any time. At the same time, levels in the hierarchy have been greatly simplified, so that promotion is a question of very short steps. A necessary condition for advancement is the continual renewal of one's professional skills, but this is not enough: at the same time, another (sufficient) condition is called for – a constant self-evaluation in relation to the international market for professional skills. In the economy of knowledge, learning takes place through the medium of people.

Work as a means of production, emancipation and social stratification is not in question, but we have to adapt ourselves, and also adapt the right of work that has been established throughout the centuries. There is, however, a great temptation to forget this and move in the direction of Anglo-Saxon practices. This would be an error. Just as erroneous would be the desire to preserve the French model at any price, but without wishing to do this one could imagine an evolution of the contract of hire which allowed for the integration of security and flexibility, of rigorous terms and the acceptance of the unexpected.

It was with this perspective in mind that in 1995 a working party under the chairmanship of Jean Boissonnat published its findings under the title of *Work in Twenty Years' Time*.[17] One of the major proposals, in response to this inevitable evolution of the contract of hire towards a simple business contract, was the creation of an overall framework to be called a *contract of activity*, which could encompass traditional contracts of hire, more flexible contracts of collaboration, periods of further training, and even periods of inactivity. This model combines flexibility of employment with a more durable respect for the skills of those employed.

This type of contract will offer an alternative to the present situation, where there is a choice between a contract of limited duration – most new appointments are of this kind – and a contract of unlimited duration. The contract of activity is a framework contract entered into by a person and a group of employers for a period of five years. Within this framework it is possible to have several successive contracts of limited duration. In this way, the transition from one period of employment to another will not be as traumatic as the position of an employee suddenly deprived of work. In addition, the cost of further training, usually measured at the moment as an average for the company as a whole, can be coupled to individual employees via the contract of activity. In this way, each person gradually builds up a sort of training credit account which can be drawn upon between contracts. Only routine and entrenched habits prevent the use of such contracts, which have already been partially tried out by several groups of employers.

Fully employed or fully active?

Work creates the wealth of our society, but it does not make it a happy one. Our society is rich indeed: today, the mean purchasing power is three times that of 1960. In France, society also shows more solidarity than many industrialized countries: more than one-half of the wealth produced is redistributed,[18] as opposed to one-third in the USA. Social justice is ensured, but the entrepreneurial spirit is threatened. A high rate of unemployment is tapping the vital economic resources of our society. Full employment would seem to be beyond our reach.

Throughout the century, increasing productivity, coupled with a reduction in working hours, has prevented any marked increase in the active section of the population. It should be added that France is among those countries in Europe with the highest birth-rate, and is therefore demographically strong.

What would a return to full employment mean today? In the past, full employment rested on the stability of companies, of careers and of trades. Now, companies are born and die, are bought and sold at an ever increasing rate. A number of jobs that are quite central today did not exist ten years ago. Full employment was also a question of the uniformity of life and the rhythms of society, of stable social patterns and styles of life. Today, diversity has replaced uniformity.

There is no doubt that what we should be aiming at is *full activity*, understood primarily as paid activity. This will be the essential way to integrate people into the workforce, because it places great emphasis on the creation of economic wealth and enables the financing of the social redistribution of wealth. At the same time, the type of contribution made by the individual will change.

Work will be increasingly a question of professional specialization, defined by specific tasks ('the mission') rather than status. This trend towards the idea of a professional mission will develop with the probable expansion of the home office. Some of us will spend part of our time working at home. All we need is a simple modem and a laptop computer. The development of the Internet is contributing to this development. '20% working time at home for 20% of those employed – this is the ideal recipe, combining the satisfaction of meeting others with the comfort of working at home made possible by technology',[19] asserts Eric Benamou, President of 3Com, a leading company in the technology of networking.

People will be distinguished by the nature of their professional mission. There will be those whose mission it is to contribute to the immediate competitiveness of the company. These will be the most numerous and the most easily interchangeable. Others will have a more strategic and permanent job, the mission of linking the company to its past and to its future. The idea of 'the personal company', launched by Bob Aubrey,[20] is gaining ground. Each person will be responsible for his or her own professional training, will carefully nurture that individual store of professional skills which makes him or her commercially attractive.

Full activity will also encompass certain activities which are unpaid today, but which will become part of the mercantile sphere. These could be personal services of various kinds, taking into account the fact that we live longer and that there is a tendency to reduce the number of working hours. All that is lacking is a market, a statutory framework and stable financing. An organization called 'Golden Age Services' (L'Age d'Or Services), which offers services to elderly and handicapped people based on the idea of a pension scheme, seems to have found the right solutions. Established by Fabrice Provin in 1991, the company and its 72 franchised partners employed 130 people in 1997 and had a turnover of 15 million francs. Other companies of this type will follow.

However, we must hope that full activity will not be limited to commercial activities. There should be room outside the sphere of paid employment for relationships and dialogue. Companies are not the sole locus of human exchange; they are but an instrument in the service of society. Having too often forgotten this, we have come to confuse work with society and the wage-earner with the citizen.

The quantum leap of mankind

The church bell rings, as it does on the hour every hour, but no one hears it. We all have our own watches, our own lives, our own time. Ancient rites are no longer the source of social life. The three basic mutations have entered our lives and have already left indelible marks. Globalization is only one of the effects they have produced, and the most recent. No doubt further inequalities will soon arise to plough even deeper furrows in our lives.

The way the world is developing is undermining the secure world of our childhood; society is breaking up into fragments, and our dreams of equality are disintegrating with it. The solid ground of work, which once gave us independence and a social network, is now giving way beneath our feet; automation is advancing so rapidly that we may begin to wonder if we are of any use at all. We are entering the era of 'all for one and every man for himself'. 'All for one' is the solidarity of a company in the face of its customer, who has to be satisfied, and kept, at any cost; 'every man for himself' is the new solitude of the producer, forced to re-examine his own skills against the yardstick of a planetary market which makes pitiless demands on levels of competence. New technologies allow the linking together of the best people in the field. Formerly, those who went with the territory were automatically on the team; today, increasingly, talent alone is what counts. And talent is only discovered if it knows how to sell itself.

From fatigue to stress [21]

We have all become workers within the economy of knowledge, whether we like it or not. Formerly, a day's work left us exhausted; today, even manual workers are not in direct contact with the materials they are working with. Very often, sales personnel do not see their customers, but only occasionally hear their voices on the phone. Increasingly, too, orders are placed by means of a silent fax, or an e-mail without mass or extension. 'Never have so few people been in direct contact with the earth, with stone, metal and other material things. This cannot but affect the way they think...', comments Jean Boissonnat in his preface to the report, *Work in Twenty Years' Time*.

One of the consequences of this revolution is that we have moved from being tired to being stressed. 'An individual is stressed when he has to make an effort to adapt to his environment', remarks Eric Albert.[22] The impression of stress is produced whenever there is a lack of alignment between the reality principle and what we would wish this reality to be. Stress is a signal, and 'stress copers' know how to use it to their advantage. Others become its victims. They live in a permanent state of suffering produced by the quantum leap, in itself an image of the constant lack of alignment between realities that succeed each other in rapid succession. They also feel the effects of the 'urgency disease' inflicted on us by the speed of change. They are afraid of losing their footing, of discovering that the skills they have so painstakingly acquired over the years are no longer of any value on the job market. In their pain they come to confuse their personal identity with their professional value. Stress is also born of the desire to control everything in a world that is more and more uncontrollable, to seek perfection when the customer simply wants immediate service, and the desire to live up to all the demands made on one.

The new face of work

Stress has replaced fatigue because work has become abstract, interactive, rapid and permanent.

- *Work is abstract*: this means that we are constantly being called upon to analyse new situations, new relationships, new pressures. Almost whatever our trade we find ourselves sitting in front of a computer. This is a far cry from the illustrations in Diderot's *Encyclopaedia*, which showed the location, tools and activities typical of each trade.[23]

- *Work is interactive*: the reduction in stocks, the necessity of responding directly and immediately to the wishes of the customer, the spatial dispersion of the different locations involved in the 'manufacture' of products or services – all these factors emphasize relationships as the binding force in this new situation of flux. Interaction has become the new matrix, and interaction implies reaction and constant awareness. One has to be ready for the sudden incursion of information, of a signal, of an order. We are far removed from the situation of the lonely artisan in the silence of his workshop; much closer, in fact, to the frenzied milling around of a restaurant kitchen. The customer is at the other side of the door: he orders what he wants, when he wants, becomes impatient, and leaves without saying a word.

- *Work is permanent*: the dividing line between work time and leisure time has become almost obliterated. The modern market space has wiped out the problem of distances and time zones. Formerly, people tried to break out of their isolation; nowadays, people are actually looking for it. A liner in the middle of the Atlantic might seem a good setting for splendid isolation, but this is not the case: you can be reached by fax, by phone, or directly over the Internet. The knowledge revolution has laid siege to our minds with no respect for working hours. Work has become intellectual, and is rather a question of preoccupation than occupation. The time in which you are actually physically present at work is less important than the results achieved. Our patterns of life are changing. Formerly, one had to walk somewhere to meet others, but in the virtual world a simple hand movement is enough to link us or isolate us. What will our immediate future be like? Virtual deserts and virtual crowds; crushed in the throng or alone and bored. Sociologists and psychiatrists are scratching their heads. Some predict a return to village life now that people can work by computer at home; others are dreaming of the global village.

However, the revolution in the market place and the economy of knowledge have only amplified a movement which began a long time ago. Because of this, the real revolution is inside ourselves. It is tearing us up and filling us with enthusiasm at the same time. Are we obsolete? Yes, if we fail to comprehend the new rules of the game. No, if we learn how to move properly, because the point is that the quantum leap is a sort of dance step. Dance, calling for harmony of movement and the tension of balance, is like life, in which body and mind are united. Dance draws together the strands of life. Today, dance is an art form, but in classical Greece it was, along with geometry, philosophy and other essential forms of knowledge, one of the major disciplines of the classical education of the whole man. Life is a dance, and the quantum leap is one of the steps. The mind makes sense of the movement, the body adds elegance to balance. The mind has understood the rules, the body prepares the action.

To understand the new rules of the global game – the development of networks and the knowledge society – means learning how to change without effort and to take up new challenges. The revolution in the market place opens up visions, concentrates efforts and globalizes all, but at the same time it diversifies and creates new forms of intelligence. The knowledge revolution makes intelligence our staple diet and globalizes ideas, but at the same time means that the craziness of the inventor, the warmth of human contacts and a meticulous attention to detail are factors as irreplaceable as they always have been.

Notes

1. *Courrier International*, No. 365, 30 October 1997.
2. Lester Thurow, *The Future of Capitalism*, London, William Morrow, 1996.
3. Daniel Cohen, *Richesse du monde, pauvretés des nations*, Paris, Flammarion, 1997, p. 126.
4. OECD, May 1997.
5. 'Competition among Nations', *UBS, International Finance*, Autumn 1993.
6. Peter Drucker, *Postcapitalist Society*, New York, HarperCollins, 1993.
7. Jean Boissonnat, preface to the report, *Le Travail dans vingt ans*, Paris, Odile Jacob, 1995.
8. *Encyclopedia Universalis*, 'Les crises économiques', 6–780.

9. Jean Boissonnat, op. cit. and Dominique Méda, *Le Travail, une valeur en voie de disparition?*, Paris, Aubier, 1995.

10. *Enquiry into the Nature and Causes of the Wealth of Nations*, 1776.

11. Jean Boissonnat, op. cit., p. 10.

12. Article 1780 of the French 'Code du travail'.

13. Jean Boissonnat, op. cit.

14. Cf. Jean-Christophe Ruffin, *La Dictature libérale*, Paris, J.-C. Lattès, 1994.

15. Dominique Méda and Juliet Schor, *Le Travail, une révolution à venir*, Paris, Arte Editions, 1997.

16. Bob Aubrey, *Le Travail après la crise*, Paris, InterEditions, 1994.

17. This commission, composed of economists, sociologists and lawyers, included two company managers, including the author.

18. 55% in 1996.

19. Europe 1, 'C'est arrivé demain', 16 November 1997 radio interview.

20. In *Le Travail après la crise,* op. cit.

21. Interview with Yves Lasfargue, *Le Monde Informatique*, Special Issue, 14 July 1995.

22. Eric Albert, *Comment devenir un bon stressé*, Paris, Odile Jacob, 1995.

23. Comparison taken from Yves Lasfargue, *Robotisés, rebelles, rejetés*, Paris, Editions de l'Atelier, 1993.

Part II
Towards the Hypertext Company

This is the era of the hypertext company.[1] A company becomes 'hypertext' in order better to serve its customers, and those who have made of it an irreplaceable instrument for the creation of services valuable to all. A 'hypertext' is a text in which the words are not merely passive. Each of them contributes to the meaning of the whole text. Each of them, at the simple click of a mouse, can open up other texts, other universes. Even so, the hypertext company is built up around the added value that is to be produced, which in turn is based on the unforeseeable links established by its customers. It is only necessary to click on the required know-how at the appropriate time in order to construct, from link to link, the product or the service called for.

The hypertext is movement: a simple 'click' leads to action. Within a company, daily activity is no longer simply repetition, reproduction or routine; instead, it is redefined at any given moment to meet or anticipate the needs of the customer, the inroads of the competition, the requirements of society. How can the daily life of a company be permanently changed without creating chaos?

The hypertext means dialogue, both in terms of the avenues it opens up and the questions it raises. Within a company today the silence indispensable to routine and rigid repetition is no longer a valid requirement. The permanent creation of new ideas calls for words, ideas, and that creative dialogue which enables everyone in the company, collectively and individually, to find a viable route towards a new reality. But how are we to make the transition from sterile debate to fruitful dialogue, from confrontation to the search for common values?

Finally, because it involves a search, *the hypertext is a learning process*. In the past, the reproduction of activities and of knowledge was a guarantee of efficiency and productivity. Today, we have to work in a different way, acquiring new forms of competence and using them to the best effect as quickly as possible. But what do we have to learn? How is our knowledge to be renewed?

Traditional companies are not well adapted to these new conditions and practices. Now is the time to build up companies that know how to change direction, without losing sight of the goals they have set themselves, of their customers, of the people and the sources of knowledge which enrich them. In short, companies which know how to be inventive, and how to evolve in a climate of uncertainty. Before becoming hypertext, however, a company has first to learn how to change, and then how to manage new sources of energy.

Notes

1. From Ikujiro Nonaka and Hirotaka Takeuchi, *The Knowledge Creating Company*, Oxford University Press, 1995.

Knowing How to Become

A SHORT TREATISE ON CHANGE

> To have the courage to change what can be changed, the serenity to accept what cannot, and the wisdom to discern one from the other.
>
> Marcus Aurelius

Vincent's firm had just been bought up. He still could not believe it. Everything had been going well; the company had been constantly growing for several years and was the admiration of all. Why had the shareholders sold out? All these questions were spinning round in his head when the manager of the group buying his company came to see him, and later he would only retain very vague memories of this meeting. The suggestions made by his interlocutor ran off him like water off a duck's back, and the reassuring tones that insisted that he would be attached to the newly formed company did not seem to be addressed to him. Vincent had not got beyond the first stage of shock and mourning.

Pierre has just been told that his company is being restructured, and that there is no place for him. In financial terms, his separation settlement is very acceptable. He is still young, and does not need to be afraid of the future. When the first moment of anger has passed he thinks about the things he has experienced with the company. Curiously enough, those who are staying on do not want to talk about it; they are too occupied trying to negotiate their future situation.

Brigitte had kept on negotiating to the bitter end. She had quickly sized up the situation: the company had no further use for her services as the accounting department she had been heading was being closed down and moved to Paris. She knew the figures and had kept her cold anger well hidden when her boss, suitably contrite, had announced to her the unavoidable necessity of reconfiguring the organization. Surprised by her determination, he had conceded more than she had hoped for, but had demanded in return that she leave the company immediately. Later, alone, she was seized by a boundless feeling of sadness.

Bertrand, the new manager of a company still in shock after having called in the receivers, has been trying for a hour to instil fresh confidence into the employees gathered in one of the workshops temporarily transformed into a conference room. Using an overhead projector, he traces the exact reasons why the company is in difficulties, presents detailed arguments for a process of reorganization, and the provisional results which might be expected to be achieved by the new strategy. No use. His words are met with nothing but incomprehension and silent defiance.

At this point, any reader could insert his or her own story of change, in the role of victim or executioner, in silence or in anger, in sorrow or the will to fight on.

And, no matter what the disaffected might say, we have already changed much. The speed of modern life, the expansion of space and the changes in social relationships have transformed our jobs, our knowledge, our daily lives at work and at home. Large slices of dogma, of previously indisputable axioms, of familiar situations and acquired habits have crumbled rapidly and irreversibly away, in fury or in silence. None of us had believed that everything could change so fast, so universally, affecting every dimension of our lives from the most simple actions and deeply rooted patterns of thought to the most entrenched of our attitudes.

On the other hand, by changing, we have learned the laws of change. We also know how to bury the past, reconstruct it with detachment and cast ourselves with passionate intensity into the shaping of new futures. Even though we are rich in information, such changes have often been painful, the process difficult and uncertain. We would like to stop now and then, have a rest, but this is hardly possible. We have also learned that change leads to more change; the balance of our daily lives is constantly upset. We may have conquered the first steps of the climb and vanquished the first slopes, but no calm plateau awaits us, no shady refuge where we can draw breath awhile.

There is a Chinese proverb that says: 'When you get to the top of the mountain, keep on climbing!' This is more than ever true today. Change is permanent and the pace is accelerating. The advent and the spread of new technologies, and the appearance of new actors on the world scene have introduced new complexities, but also new possibil- ities – a multitude of possible futures which are going to be in compe- tition. We have to judge, choose, decide and act for ourselves, constructing our own destinies before other people do it for us.

We have learned to change, and now we have to learn how to become. The word 'change', much used and much abused, no longer expresses what is really at stake. It expresses very well the necessity of adaptation and reaction; it signifies the transformation that is called for, but in the end it is a defensive verb. And the changes facing us today are so profound that defence alone is not sufficient. We are forced to find other verbs that can express the voluntary, proactive and imaginative response which these changes call for. To know how to change is a necessary condition for survival, but knowing how to become means being able to extract oneself from one situation in order to create another, just as the famous Baron Münchhausen did in the course of his picaresque adventures.

> On another occasion I set about to jump across a pond, but when I was in the middle of my leap I perceived that it was wider than I had thought at first: so I turned my horse round in the middle of its flight and returned to the edge of the pond from which I had jumped, to make a new attempt. However, on the second occasion I fared no better and fell into the pond up to my neck: I would surely have perished if I had not by the strength of my arms been able to lift myself up with my own pigtail, both me and my horse, which I grasped firmly between my knees.[1]

Knowing how to become means first of all being aware of the rules governing change in daily life. But it also means being aware of the factors that allow daily life itself to be changed.

The two cultures of change

The most visible changes are those that take place in organizations. The rules of the game would seem to be clear: change occurs when the balance between the wishes of the actors and the constraints of the environment is disturbed. A company is first and foremost built on the wishes of the shareholders, of the leadership and of the employees, who together mobilize the resources necessary to create the added value which makes the company competitive; their choices, the measure of their efforts and their attitude are the object of the strategic

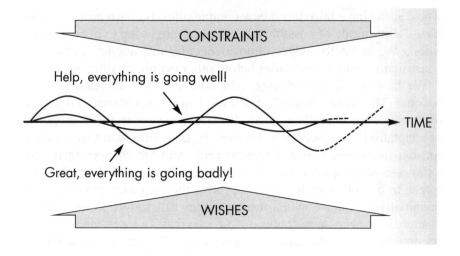

decisions made by the company. The company must also reckon with the wishes of other actors: its customers, its suppliers, its commercial allies, its competitors. Generally, the company knows these people well, but even so often ignores the future actors who might enter the game: competitors from far away, suppliers suddenly become competitors. All will have an impact, often unforeseeable, on the development of the game.

As to the constraints, the list is almost endless: environmental or financial, technological and sociological developments, laws, norms and regulations. There is a chart, or map, to guide the progress of the game, and a certain understanding of it, but very often there is no clear idea of where the chart may lead. And even when people think they can discern new constellations of power, new data, they do not always make use of this insight and are taken by surprise. This is no doubt why there are at least two major ways of tackling change.

'Great, everything is going badly!'

The first type of change, the most spectacular one, is undoubtedly the most widespread. This is intermittent change. It attacks all kinds of companies – solid or shaky, large or small. Some, by virtue of their social entrenchment, seem built to defy eternity. Other have experienced a regular progression: their share indices attract the holders of better portfolios. For the most part, the years pass uneventfully. Certainties become entrenched, profits rise. Yet, suddenly, results can plummet, recession sets in. The veil of habit is torn away. Analysts discover that firms formerly presented as models are now falling behind; their products are obsolete, their factories antiquated. Customers have been aware of this for a long time, and the most faithful of them have quietly departed without attracting attention. Business allies are dispirited, but quietly await developments. The management, anaesthetized by routine, have noticed nothing. Then, suddenly, things happen quickly: share prices plunge, the board appoints a new managing director; firings, thinning out, strategic reorganization... all the moves that should have been made years before are implemented in the course of a few weeks. The new boss 'rocks the boat a bit', passes copious judgement on his predecessor. The fall has been heavy, but this only makes prospects for the future more rosy: 'Great, everything is going badly', he thinks, 'this crisis gives me a free hand and maximum power.' The company, severely wounded, swallows the bitter pill.

'Help, everything is going well!'

There is another and more discrete way of changing. The companies that practise it are like the others, but often less glamorous, less spectacular. Following a policy of constant change, they endure and survive for decades without making waves. They are always in front, or perhaps just never really behind, and seem to ride the surf of change without effort. Their managers are modest people, worriers

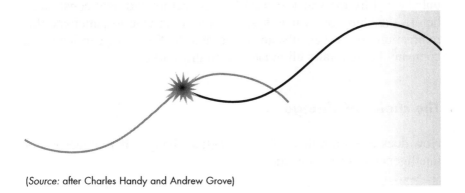

(*Source:* after Charles Handy and Andrew Grove)

even; they are always calling their organization into question, expressing doubts about its efficacy every day. They are constantly revising the chart of change, guessing who might be new competitors, anticipating new norms, and despite all their success they often have more questions in their heads than ready-made answers. Their rallying cry will therefore be: 'Help! Everything is going well, let us not be lulled to sleep or distracted by our success.'

If we are to choose between these two approaches to change, the second is the best – more progressive, but clearly more painful. Perpetual change calls for energy and concentration all the time.

Perpetual change calls for the ability to recognize the roots of change, to know how to find the *point of redirection*. This point of redirection, which is a point in time and the very nub of perpetual change, is also the point of no return in relation to intermittent change.

Starting at this point an S-shaped curve develops. This curve is that of life: it starts slowly, gains in strength, reaches its apogee and then declines gradually. The secret of change is linked to the capacity to be able to start afresh from a new point of departure, moving on another growth curve. This point of departure, the point of redirection, is born close to the apogee of the 'current' life curve, a moment which is normally permeated with a quiet feeling of plenitude rather than the raising of disturbing questions, a fact which makes it difficult at such a point to think about changing steeds – that is, one's life – at all. Perpetual change means being able to recognize this point and having the courage to change, utilizing all the resources and the relaxed strength of the apogee of a cycle soon to begin its decline.

When talking about a company, this point of redirection is 'strategic':[2] it is the point at which the hitherto stable system becomes unbalanced by the shock caused by new actors and new constraints, before sketching out a new system. Not being able to anticipate this redirection, and especially not being able to follow it, can lead to a company being totally eliminated from the market.

The choice of change

How does one learn this skill of perpetual change? Is it a question of intelligence or of organization?

It is no use making use of intelligence in the 'intellectual' sense; how many statesmen have there not been, and brilliant, even visionary, leaders, who have passed by major changes without even seeing them? If it is a question of intelligence, then we are talking about an integrative intelligence, which ties into the present, integrating subtle changes which the busy observer will not notice. Does this imply a lack of will? We do not seem to be lucidly clear until some crisis opens our mind and reality imposes itself brutally upon us. Companies which only change every ten years in a spectacular and painful manner are paying the price for having disregarded the reality which was trying to impose itself at an earlier stage. Despite such setbacks, it is likely that the company will continue to practise intermittent change because it simply does not know how to practise the rigorous discipline of slow, daily change.

The fact is that we have short memories. As the French proverb says: 'the scalded cat fears cold water!' In other words, if we keep on reproducing the same errors, this is because we can only see what is familiar to us. Change is right beneath our eyes, but our brains are focused on familiar mental schemata, and for this reason the signs of a new situation, embryonic and not at all spectacular, pass unnoticed. The image they project does not correspond to anything familiar – and therefore we ignore it.

We are moreover the plaything of our emotions. If we would only agree to take an objective view of the real world, we would more easily be able to change. But we cannot and will not see anything which puts our feelings at stake. So it is with the intermittent change which characterizes those companies whose development has been crowned with success and which refuse to see the collapse of their markets, sensing that this would demand sacrifices, a tightening of financial policy and the abandonment of an offensive style – all kinds of perceivable suffering which people do not want to live through and therefore hide from. This explains more often than one might imagine the recession into which change forces many companies.

Above all, we are blind. We only see what corresponds to our vision of the future. It is said that trees do not grow up to the sky, but there are many companies whose strategy incorporates a linear vision of the future. The stock market crash of 1987, like the collapse of Asian economies ten years later, appear, in retrospect, as inevitable, and yet most of us were taken by surprise. Hence the interest in constantly advancing probable scenarios. Rather than simply bowing one's head to the future in advance, one poses the question: if our competitor does such and such, how am I going to react? By constructing these different hypotheses in one's head, one ends up by structuring a 'memory of the future'.

Finally, we generally tend to believe that we can change people by simply changing organizations, and, correspondingly, that changing people's behaviour will quickly transform organizations. Yet reality is contrary: by slowing down the rate of change in organizations, we render change more difficult; and by speeding up the rate of change in people we jump over those essential steps which by constructing a future they are not involved in will prevent them from identifying themselves with it. Learning how to become is something that both people and organizations have to work at, since perpetual change is not possible unless people and companies change simultaneously and together. In other words, change must not be viewed exclusively from the point of view of organizations, or of people, but has to be conceived of within the dialectical relationship that binds them together in practice.

Intelligence and memory, emotion and will, reason, organization and feelings are the unavoidable protagonists in the process of change. Are we the masters of these factors, or their slaves?

Reason and feelings

No organization changes of its own accord. It forms both the framework and the refuge of the games people play, but cannot change unless they change it and then accommodate themselves to the new situation.

Feelings: the five stages

Whether it takes place gradually or suddenly, change is a rupture with the past. The present situation has to be abandoned in favour of an uncertain future. One vaguely recognizes that the change will be irreversible; but at the same time one hangs on to the tattered remnants of the present, already endowed with the colours and savours of paradise lost. To change means to go into mourning for the reality which is disappearing in order to take up a new life, very similar and yet very different. Psychiatrists, psychologists and sociologists, who are familiar with the stages of the process of mourning, divide the process of alteration into five stages. Without knowing it, we go through these stages in our personal lives, in our companies, in social life.

Denial

The first stage of change is simply a refusal to see that anything has changed at all. At this point we are at the root of change, at the point of strategic redirection. Certain aspects of our environment have indeed been modified, but as yet the possible consequences of these modifications are hard to perceive, and it is still easy to avoid seeing that any change has taken place. The moment of denial is a sort of reflex reaction – when learning about an accident or the death of someone close: 'It can't be true!' Those who in the business world have experienced a bankruptcy, a change of stockholders or an economic recession will be able to remember that their first reaction was one of incredulity. This stage may last for a longer or shorter time, as long as the changes are not clearly manifest. Often, a combination of proposals meant to soothe the pain, of empty phrases and of diplomacy, end up by making us forget the change which in fact has taken place, but these strategies of temporization, of appeasement and soothing medication soon cease to work when the second stage arrives.

Anger

The second stage is violent: a shout of rage, a manifestation of resistance, a laying down of tools. Take an example of a company in the foodstuffs industry, whose leading product is suddenly threatened by a competitor. The management works out a plan of investment and massive reorganization, a coherent plan based on solid arguments aiming to recapture the lost market sectors by a programme of massive investment in production machinery. Moreover, it is the proud intention of the management to avoid redundancies. This phase of analysis, carried out in secret, lasts for several months, and when the necessary studies have been made and the decisions taken a team of consultants is called in to put the financial plan into action. For several weeks, everything goes according to plan; the employees are co-operative. Then suddenly, one day, there is a strike. Motivated by a

desire to tread softly, the management has made little effort to communicate the importance of change. The plans which they are trying to implement were originally a response to questions posed by themselves alone. The employees at the factory have not been involved either in the question or in the response. Incredulity has given place to anger. The strike lasts for one day, long enough to provide explanations, to get the employees to see the risks being run by the company, and the necessity of rapidly making the new investments. The employees go back to work, but now there is an open wound. No one really believed the promises made; all the employees were convinced that there would be redundancies. The future will prove them wrong, but they have lost confidence in the management.

Anger is an expression of powerlessness in the face of unforeseen change. It is a necessary stage in the process of mourning. Can it be avoided? Certainly not; we need to let our emotions run free, and to do so as soon as possible, as close to the events of daily life as possible. In companies involved in perpetual change, one is struck by the passion, even the violence of the discussions. Events are commented on, avidly discussed. This allows everyone to pass through the moment of anger, a testimony to impotence, moving on towards a gradual and negotiated acceptance of the new situation.

Negotiation

The process of negotiation, trading, marks the third stage. It is a question of negotiating the cost of change, and first of all of assigning responsibility: is one a victim or a culprit? This stage is characterized by a movement to and fro between the indignant anger of the victim and the guilty silence of the culprit. As the pendulum swings back and forth the balance of forces changes. At the end of the day, instead of exhausting itself trying to identify victims and culprits, the process of negotiation settles down. At first, change is accepted as long as nothing is really changed, or almost nothing. If 'nothing' is out of reach, one hopes that the 'almost nothing' will be as little as possible. By analogy with real mourning, one reconstructs the presence of the deceased, who is perfect in all ways, except for the possession of life. In a company this toing and froing is often a laborious business; one has to accept that some take a step backwards, while others state their conditions for change. Sometimes, one is thrown back to the previous stage, but in the end even the most nostalgic find their position insupportable and artificial. Why hang on to one's office, one's title and position if change has made them void of content; why continue to keep up appearances? Finally, the routine of daily life reasserts itself, and passions abate. The fourth stage begins.

Sadness

This is the stage of feeling down, even depressed. The negotiating is over. The mourning is complete, one has lived it out in full. One has not yet begun to invest one's energy in the new reality, and one only sees the unpleasant things, but one knows that the situation is irreversible. One only requires the time to adjust oneself. This stage can last a long time and is often punctuated by 'funeral rites': monologues drawing up the long list of changes, without animosity, but with the sad certainty that those who regret them are in a minority. There are moments of sadness when the complete list opens before one like a void, and moments of fear in the face of this void without any familiar landmarks. This is a delicate period, and any kind of victory communiqué on the part of the new leaders – in the case of a take-over, for instance – will be seen as an affront by those directly affected by the changes.

The new start

The fifth stage marks a new beginning. The earlier situation has not been forgotten, it is just not relevant any longer. One look around reveals how much things have changed: the company has changed its name; the first batch of new products has left the production line; new customers have replaced the old ones. Work is not the same as it was before. New professional skills have been developed. Beneath it all, one remains the same, but it has taken a lot of changing to reach this point.

These stages are simply described, perhaps even over-simplified, but they are unavoidable. One might be able to speed them up, but none of them can be jumped over, and to ignore this fact entails the risk of going round and round in the process of change. How long does it take to pass through these five stages? This depends on the extent of change involved, but the specialists say six to eight months, although some of those with experience say it can take up to two years. At the same time it is necessary to allow the emotional clock to adjust to that of the organization, to swing in tune with the process of change without blocking or stopping it.

Jean-Louis Roy, Professor of Management Theory at Essec, has reduced this process to three stages,[3] a sort of waltz in three-four time between the people and the organization. The first period is a mixture of the old organization and the attachment which people feel to it, both by habit and conviction. The second period involves the destruction of the organization and the wrench that this entails. Finally, there is the reconstruction of a new organization within which people will gradually come to feel at home, after definitively breaking the bonds that bound them to the defunct organization. Who has not danced this stationary dance – in his present company or the previous one – accompanied by internal developments sometimes of great violence?

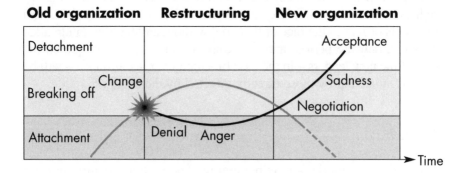

Source: after Jean-Louis Roy and Brain Technologies Corp.

Reason: the three levers

The waltz of change is not silent. It is noisy and full of dissonance, a tumult of words with contradictory meanings, a maelstrom of inverted images. Each person only hears what he wants to hear, sees what he wants to see; one man's heavy rain cloud is described by another as blazing sunshine. To see and to hear – images and words are important.

Images. First and foremost, changing a company means finding an image, a metaphor for the new reality. This new reality is the cloud that surrounds us, the obstacle that rises up before us; we have to construct an image which turns this formless and menacing shadow into a mountain with a precise shape and contours. It is a large mountain, but it can be climbed. It is a matter of describing the mountain in such a way as to ensure that those who are going to make the climb with you can actually see it. A few years ago, in an attempt to raise standards of quality, Renault placed near their assembly lines examples of models produced by their competitors to provide a standard of comparison. In other words, the change that was called for was not something vague and far away; it was a concrete image, become a familiar fact of daily life.

Words. It is necessary to find those who have described the path to take in order to ascend the mountain. 'We have not received the Earth from our parents, but have merely borrowed it from our children.' This wonderful phrase of Saint-Exupéry might help to get a company started on a sincere policy of concern for the environment, to establish procedures, achieve the necessary certifications, and so on. Such rational steps support and mark out the path of hesitant progress towards the unknown. A rational analysis of the situation, which is indispensable, cannot replace the image which is, precisely – irreplaceable. The image creates and describes the mountain; the words construct and mark out the way.

Change has two languages: on the one hand a rational, analytic, verbal language, and on the other hand an analogue language, metaphorical, symbolic and 'silent'. Rationality belongs to the left side of the brain, as does excessive stiffness in the face of change. Intuition is attributed to the right hemisphere, but also the excessive confidence that comes from dreams. Bob Lutz, former President of the

Chrysler Corporation, insists on the irrational, imaginative and innovative element when thinking about the customer:

> Analysis and quantitative approaches are products of the left side of the brain, and they have often made us ignore the forest that lies hidden behind all these trees so carefully cultivated by the refined methods of quantitative analysis. My crusade at Chrysler was to reinstate the right half of the brain. To the left-brain thinker, the automobile industry is a science, and indeed it is; but it is not just that, because nobody buys a car or a truck on the basis of a purely rational decision.[4]

We have to learn to speak the two languages of change, to draw on our two brain hemispheres and the specific languages they use.

> To translate the reality perceived, thus synthesizing in an image our experience of the world, is without doubt a function of the right hemisphere. To the left hemisphere is probably assigned the task of rationalizing this image, of dividing its totality into subject and object; the task of reifying the reality as well as drawing from it what seem to be the ineluctable consequences. These consequences in their turn consolidate the image, setting in motion a self-justifying process which proceeds until the moment when no contradictory factor can modify the image, but only serve to refine and improve it.[5]

Yet how to find exactly the right term, and present just that image which summarizes the situation and shows the way to proceed, this is a problem that has been called 'the burden of words, the shock of the photograph',[6] a slogan which directly illustrates the double language of change. Those who have decided on change have previously created for themselves an interior image, but very often they then make use of a language that appeals to the reason of those who have no reason to believe any more, instead of opening up for them the image of a new dream and a new way forward. Others may use the language of metaphor but are deaf to those who are waiting for an explanation of the situation and new reasons to believe in the future. In some cases, when one part of ourselves receives images, the other part cannot make sense of them; meaning disappears if the image is blurred. The right brain makes the decisions, the left analyses them, but if the right brain sees something new, the left brain will make a thorough analysis and decree that it cannot be true. Which of us has never faced difficulties of communication? One describes the rosy future in passionate and flowery language, and suddenly one of the listeners demands to know: 'Well, how does that work out in practice?' On the other hand, one remembers the spark that lit up in the eyes of a listener whom you have just presented with an image that really struck home, revealing in a few seconds what any amount of well-documented reports have failed to reveal.

We need both sides of the brain, and the default of one produces a profound imbalance. This can be illustrated by the case of Phineas Gage.[7] In the summer of 1848, an explosion to clear some rocks in connection with the building of a railway in Vermont smashed an iron bar through his skull. Not only did the young foreman survive, but his clarity of mind was in no way affected by the loss of part of his right brain. On the other hand, his personality had changed: he had become asocial, without emotions, no longer capable of making the smallest decision based on feelings. Reason and feelings are inseparable; intelligence needs the emotions to make decisions. It is, however, the case that there are fewer links between the right and left hemispheres than there are within each hemisphere.[8] In the case of a crisis, of a sudden break or rapid change, this dichotomy may pose problems. The left brain may interpret information differently than the right brain; the language of the body may be in conflict with the language of words. If this is true of individuals, it is undoubtedly also true of groups. In a company, schizophrenia quickly spreads if the language officially used is belied by behaviour.

Paul Watzlawick, psychiatrist and researcher at the Institute of Palo Alto, has studied these phenomena in patients for a long time. He has proposed to practitioners three techniques based on the different reactions to change of the two halves of our brains. The purpose of these techniques is to manage the conflict between the two hemispheres. Can they be transposed to the world of organizations? A company is of course composed of people, but as such it has no right or left brain. At the risk of making an invalid application of the ideas, one cannot help noticing that the three levers proposed by Watzlawick evoke a lot of experiences familiar from the corporate world.

The first lever

This is a question of using to the full the right half of the brain and its capacity to grasp complex situations at a glance. In order to do this we have to speak its language: the language of metaphor, analogy and humour. Advertisers are our best guides along this road; the power of a single image, a simple play on words is enough to change the whole image of a company in the mind of the consumer. The language of the right brain is figurative, the language of dreams and of poetry. It is the seat of humour, of understatement, of the play on words, all effective tools of change that can undermine and destroy the most rational of classifications. 'With a sovereign disregard for the limits of logic and rationality, one insightful phrase can fragment the accepted images of the world and become an agent of change.' The right brain can indeed see, but its images are not very precise; it prefers to reconstruct reality on the basis of some tiny but essential element: a smell, a few bars of music, a minimal gesture, the barest of outlines evokes a place, a situation or a face, and is enough to reconstruct a new reality.

What can such language do to change a company? In the first place, acceptance of the fact that one image is worth a thousand words, and that it is not enough to entrench oneself behind figures, statements and points of view. To consider humour as an inconvenience, to despise intuition and the disorder of the fair, to believe only in facts – these are all effective ways of banning the right brain from a company, effective ways of silencing the most effective of the languages of change. Companies that cannot adjust to perpetual change have, so to speak, been deserted by the right hemisphere. Instead of daring to take a new look at things, they cling to a superannuated image of reality, but one that is so imprinted in their minds, so rationalized and intellectualized that they cannot get rid of it. No new reality, however insistent, can stand its ground in the face of their impeccable logic. Accustomed to defending their corporate body they have become 'ideological', that is, their basic 'idea' (in the Greek sense of 'image') is shaped by logic, and no new perception which might bring the official analysis into question will be accepted.

There are a thousand ways of cultivating the right hemisphere in a company. Apart from images, art must be used in all its forms: exhibitions of paintings, sculpture, theatre, music – all work to transform, for an evening in the first place, but also in the long run, those places normally reserved for the rational procedures of the left brain. Cultivating the right brain of a company ensures that the structure of the organization is in balance between the rational and the intuitive. It is a question of allowing the multiple languages that each recount their own vision of the world to develop and to interact. It is a question of forbidding meetings which only assemble those who resemble each other, and the only outcome of which is an ever stronger affirmation of those certainties which are already deeply rooted. Cultivating the right brain of a company means starting off as often as possible by neutralizing all excesses of rationalism, and this in fact is the second lever used by Watzlawick to heal patients whose image of the world has made them ill.

The second lever

The struggle between the left and right hemispheres of the brain is an unequal one. The rational side too easily carries the day. The right brain holds a global perception of reality, but with little attention to detail or precision, and for this reason it is impotent in the face of the imperious logic of the left brain, its analyses, reasonings and impressive power of argument. Neutralizing the left hemisphere permits access to the right. The methods to achieve this are numerous and make use of the reflexes of the left brain while turning them aside. The left brain is reasonable and logical. It does not like asymmetry or uncertainty and is blocked by contradictory signals, by paradoxes which question the classical dichotomy of rational analyses. Certain kinds of injunction make us petrified: 'be happy!', 'be spontaneous!', 'be creative!', 'change!' Paradoxically, such injunctions often plunge us into great confusion; how can we force ourselves to do something which should be spontaneous and effortless? The more we try to be inventive or to change, the less we achieve, like 'the insomniac who tries to achieve the spontaneous phenomenon of sleep by an effort of will'. Real change is a spontaneous act and often takes place unawares. Trying to programme it actually impedes it.

How do we get out of this impasse? One might attempt to 'treat the symptom'. Take the example of a wife who, convinced that her husband does not love her any more, nags at him, saying: 'I know you don't love me any more. You're going to leave me...' Her husband protests that he does love her, but it makes no difference. Their analyst, rather than attacking the problem, decides to attack the symptoms – the above exchange of question and answer – and asks the husband to reply next time, smiling: 'That's right, I don't love you and I'm going to leave you.' By stating the 'solution' that the wife fears, that is, the departure of her husband, they lay a trap for the left hemisphere. In a company, reassuring those who are afraid of change by using consoling words may often in itself prevent the process of change.

In general, the dialectical approach is a tool for blocking the left brain, plunging the person one is talking to into the impasse of the false alternative: 'Heads I win, tails you lose!' This is undoubtedly why some organizational consultants when faced with a company in a crisis work out a programme of action so complicated that those involved, by common accord, end up preferring the painful but simple solution they were trying to avoid. Above all, opening the route to the right brain means pushing through the cul-de-sac in which our reason has got itself trapped. This is what Alexander the Great did when he cut the Gordian knot. In the temple of Gordium in Asia Minor there was a famous rope that bound the yoke of the chariot of King Gordias to the wagon pole. It was the subject of a prophecy: he who could untie it would become the master of Asia. Alexander the Great tried to untie it without success, so in the end he cut through it with his sword. This is the technique that is called 'stepping back out of the frame', moving out of the picture to form a new image of reality.

The third lever

'If you want to see, learn to act.'[9] This aphorism summarizes the third technique which makes use of action as a tool to circumnavigate the left brain and open up the right. It comes down to creating change by action.

The most frequently used technique is undoubtedly the *pre-emptive approach*, a technique familiar to the rhetoricians of old, which consists in anticipating the criticism or resistance of another by turning it to one's own advantage. For example, when faced with an impasse, one might say: 'Well, there is one way out of this, but the very simplicity of the solution will probably make you turn it down'; or: 'I have an idea, but you are going to find it ridiculous'; or yet again: 'I'm a bit afraid of your reaction, so I'm a bit hesitant about proposing this solution.'

Another technique, the *provocative prohibition*, consists in reserving the right to change to certain carefully selected people, whose curiosity, jealousy or the desire to imitate do the rest. This is the way in which Antoine Parmentier, an apothecary in the king's army, was able in 1785 to encourage French peasants to grow potatoes. To incite the covetousness of the farmers, he had the field at Sablons where he had planted the precious roots guarded by day but not by night. Until the time of this very cleverly designed 'publicity campaign', no one had succeeded in developing the cultivation of the potato, which had been introduced into France in 1616, but forbidden by the authorities in 1630 (the plant was thought to bring the plague!).

Finally, the *technique of the challenge* is a strong incentive to action: 'We could do this, but we would never be able to manage it in time!'; 'We shall have to reduce production costs on this product, but that's impossible, isn't it?' This is what Bertrand Martin did in 1984 in the case of the New Sulzer company, which was on the edge of bankruptcy. The employees, who were not used to change, were unaware of the extent of the danger, and of the influence they might have on its destiny. Bertrand Martin decided to tell them the truth and present them with the challenge of putting the company on the right path. Each employee, in connection with his or her own job, suggested ways of economizing or of increasing production. The company soon began to make money again and conquered new markets. The employees had truly picked up the gauntlet.[10]

This third lever reveals the limits of change which is limited to thought alone, whether right or left brain. The quantum leap is more than anything a dance step, in which body and mind are one. The 'virtualization' of our daily lives should not make us forget the importance of such phenomena as a meeting, a gesture, a look. The tools of virtual reality may extend our senses, permitting us to see and hear at a distance, but cannot replace them. The book cannot replace the journey.

Knowing how to become: the meta-rules

Knowing how to become means mastering the rules that allow us to change daily life, to extract ourselves from the pond like Baron Münchhausen. How can we discover these rules, these meta-rules, which will allow us to replace the rules we normally live by?

The analysis of crises is a powerful tool in this connection. In 1993, the Association for Progress in Management[11] gathered a group of top managers of all kinds. The aim of this working group was to arrive at a better understanding of why certain companies came through crises unscathed, whereas others stumbled, or went down. Not having any clear blueprint to work from, the group analysed three major lines of behaviour, three meta-rules, which might help to explain the success of these companies.

Seeing things earlier: the time of the signs

In the first place, these companies have been able to change without too much effort because they have been able to see sooner than others the point of redirection which signals change. Seeing things earlier is the first meta-rule, and means integrating the right brain into the workings of the company. The companies studied revealed a sort of clairvoyance, based on the broad and systematic application of various techniques involving anticipation, watchfulness, the evaluation of performance, and comparison with the best in the field. Thanks to these techniques, they had developed the habit of picking up those weak signals indicating approaching change which we have referred to earlier. Seeing things earlier than others means introducing the future into the daily thinking of the company. This is a difficult exercise in those organizations which can only see the future in the form of reduced investments, and even more difficult in those where the management spends so much time reporting what has happened in the past that they have no time to look ahead and beyond. Seeing things earlier means giving the company's five senses free rein. This takes time, and calls for a panoramic vision. What is seen must also be widely disseminated.

Mastering this first meta-rule means bringing the future into the present, but how much time should be reserved for the future? This is the question posed by Gary Hamel[12] and C. K. Pralahad to the leaders and managers of major companies. The answers are disquieting: only 40% of their time is spent on the external activities of the company, and of this only 30% on the future. In other words, at this level top leaders only spend 12% of their time on the future, but this is not all. A company's vision of the future cannot be measured by the clairvoyance of the leadership alone; they have to share this new idea of the future with the employees. The verdict of the investigation is implacable: hardly 20% of the time spent on the future is spent on sharing it with the rest of the company. This means that at the end of the day the leaders only spend a meagre 2% of their time discussing their vision of the future with the employees.

This analysis does not mean that the employees working under these leaders are not oriented towards the future. The point is that no matter how much time they spend on the future, the company does not benefit from it, because only the time spent on sharing future visions – the 2% offered by the leaders – will have any impact on the total activity of the company. The conclusion of the exercise is ineluctable: the problems of today derive essentially from the fact that too little time was spent yesterday on observing and constructing the future.

Acting more quickly: the time for learning

It is not enough to see change coming before others, one has to take advantage of it before others do. The rapid exploitation of information is an obvious competitive advantage. In an information society, being the first to take advantage of an opportunity offered can be decisive, and being able to make rapid use of information that has been gathered requires the company to be geared up to this. Acting more quickly means finding the type of realization and action called for by the new image. It is a question of reconciling the senses (right hemisphere) and analysis (left hemisphere). It involves the diffusion and rapid learning of new data and the consequences it may lead to. Those companies that had survived a crisis had been able, more rapidly than others, to reach concrete conclusions based on the changes looming over the horizon. This point is fundamental. Many companies, especially the large ones, are richly provided with studies and analysis. On paper, they have all the means enabling them to see before others do, but what do they use this information for? It is not uncommon to discover that expensive studies have never been exploited, and the reason is often simple: these studies presented a view so different from that constructed by the organization that it was found preferable to ignore them.

In contrast, those companies who knew how to change immediately set about learning new skills and experimenting with new practices in the light of the new perceptions and tendencies thus revealed. Gradually, the lessons from such experimentation came to form a common pool of knowledge, competences and modes of operation.

Reorganize: the time for innovation

By seeing things differently, by acquiring new knowledge, by establishing new ways of working, one ends up registering that the company has changed, and in a radical manner. Reorganizing means inventing both the foundation and the expression of the new reality which has been created together, and which in no way resembles the preceding reality and the type of organization this entailed. On the bottom line of behaviour, the reaction of these companies to changes both foreshadowed and experienced was usually completely original. A new mode of organization established itself. Take the example of Potain, a company that built machines for public works. Confronted by extraordinary shifts in the market, the company succeeded in making variable most of the expenses normally regarded as fixed, including insurance contracts, by indexing them to the company's profit and loss figures. The case of Sidel[13] is also well known, today one of the high-flyers on the French stock market, and one of the guinea pigs used in this study: in the context of a world market glutted with machinery and showing exponential but unpredictable growth, this company was able to maintain an astoundingly low level of expenditure by co-operating with subcontractors who constructed the machines designed in its workshops.

On each occasion, the responses to these new challenges were innovative, and at all events different from the classical, and indeed predictable responses which their less fortunate competitors were able to mobilize. This ability to implement original solutions emphasized the importance of the right brain in the organization of the company, the ability to organize creativity and the use of intuition.

How can these meta-rules be introduced into companies used to perpetual change? Jacques Lefèvre, an expert in reviving companies in the Philips group, has outlined a three-stage procedure, which has been reproduced in the preceding paragraphs.

The first stage, the time of signs, calls for imagination and authority. In effect it is a question of identifying the signs that announce change and diffusing them as soon as possible within the company. Managing these signs means awakening the right brain of the company which has languished, turned to stone, in a prison of rationality. It is a question of knowing how to use the three levers described above. One must not expect anything of the company in

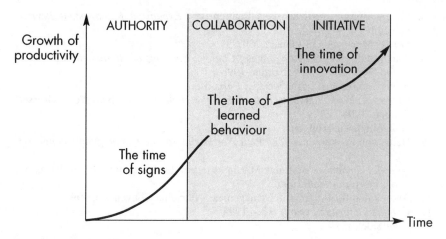

Source: after Jacques Lefèvre

terms of productivity; rather, one must allow the images to worm their way into the minds of the employees.

The second stage, acting earlier, requires that new knowledge and new behaviour be mobilized as fast as possible, and in order to do this collaboration and teamwork are essential. The effect of such learning processes is quickly seen. Productivity increases. The company reaps the fruits of change.

The third stage should be engaged when productivity is at its height. The knowledge and patterns of behaviour that have been acquired are no use any more. The effect of learning quickly leads to results. Inventiveness is called for again, the collective right brain must be turned on at full power.

The meta-rules are now in place and guide the movement of the company, expected or unexpected, but exploding with energy. Some of these movements will be familiar, others yet unused will turn out to be essential.

Notes

1. Quoted by Paul Watzlawick in *Munchhausen's Pigtail, or Psychotherapy and 'Reality' Essays and Lectures*, New York, W.W. Norton, May 1990.
2. Andrew Grove, *Only the Paranoid Survive*, New York, Currency Doubleday, 1996.

3. In 'De l'usage du deuil dans l'entreprise', *Expansion Management Review*, September 1997.
4. *Forbes Magazine*, 13 January 1997.
5. Paul Watzlawick, *The Language of Change: Elements of Therapeutic Communication*, New York, W.W. Norton, 1993.
6. Advertising slogan of the weekly, *Paris-Match*.
7. Descartes' *Error, Emotion, Reason and the Human Brain*, New York, Grosset/ Pútman, 1994.
8. Paul Watzlawick, op. cit.
9. Heinz von Forster, quoted by Paul Watzlawick in *The Language of Change,* op. cit.
10. *Oser la confiance*, Bertrand Martin, Vincent Lenhardt and Bruno Jarrosson, Paris, Insep Editions, 1996.
11. Association for Progress in Management, Marseille Convention, 1993.
12. *Competing for the Future*, HBS, 1994.
13. www.sidel.fr.

6 The Fruit is Blind, only the Tree can See

THE THREE ENERGIES

> The future is only a question of putting the past in order, you don't have to foresee it, only allow it to happen.
>
> Antoine de Saint-Exupéry

A company is a tree, and by its fruit it shall be known. There are a number of 'fruits' that bear witness to the vitality of the tree and are necessary signs of change in progress: finding answers to essential questions before others do; acting faster than the others to implement change; inventing new kinds of organization to enable such action. These fruits are fluid and silky, like speed, weighty as action, warm in hue like the glow of efficiency, and possess the unmistakable taste of innovation.

And yet: 'The fruit is blind, only the tree can see.'[1] Understanding the situation and adapting to it is not enough. The fruit is but the product of the tree, drawing its vital force from essential sources of energy in the tree which allow it to grow and develop. What are these sources of energy?

First of all, there is *the energy of our customers*. This is the company's premier source of energy, composed of the added value of sales, pride in being able to serve, and the information regarding the know-how which has to be mobilized to gain their confidence today and that needs to be developed to maintain it tomorrow. This energy, given by the customers without regard to who is able to listen to them, to observe and respect them, is inaccessible to those who have not added to their traditional know-how two new talents: knowing how to see and knowing how to relate.

Knowing how to see no longer means offering a lifeless object or a blind service, but entering into the thinking of the customer, searching out the hidden needs which you will be able to transform into a service that matches

117

them exactly. Knowing how to relate means unrelentingly meeting the customer on his own ground, forming an alliance that is a far cry from the old strategy of 'conquer and forget' and much closer to an approach based on co-operation and loyalty.

Second, there is the energy of our employees – the main source of tomorrow's energy, some will say. Once more, it is a question of transforming human resources into energy. It is often the case that reorganization due to some crisis or other stifles initiative. Innovation dies off and energy disappears into thin air when training programmes are deferred and bonus arrangements are not renewed. Energy also disappears even when people are simply measured by what they cost the organization, the extent to which they increase the cost of an operation, rather than by the profits and skills they bring with them. Even though the value of a company always depends on the assets listed in the accounts, it depends even more on the way these assets are used – and this is a question of the irreplaceable know-how of the employees, an asset which does not figure on the books. If this asset is not nurtured, the company is in danger of finding itself bereft of energy when the upswing finally comes...

Finally, there is the energy of our organizations. Constructed to provide a clear framework and a means of control, our old organizational structures are badly adapted to the freedom called for by a culture of intelligence, which in order to bear fruit needs time to create, space to manoeuvre and interaction with others. Wishing to create too much order, they have ended up by extinguishing the vital force.

Company managers can only get their organizations moving again by sharing power and initiative with their employees. If in addition they then learn how to organize their companies around these indispensable sources of energy, their own authority will emerge reinforced, and their power will be strengthened. These sources of energy are inexhaustible, but fragile; they are self-renewing, but wither away if ignored.

This text appeared in the magazine, *L'Entreprise*, in February 1992. Since that time, these intuitions have been further refined, and the knowledge economy has become increasingly important. Company organization has also evolved, taking account of these sources of energy, now seen to be essential. Today, they constitute a company's most precious possession, its intelligence capital.

If Adam Smith should return

If Adam Smith should return from the grave, he would undoubtedly add intelligence capital to his list of factors essential to production. At the time when he wrote his *Inquiry into the Nature and Causes of the Wealth of Nations* (1776), the basic source of wealth was land and property. His revolutionary idea was to state that apart from land and the wealth produced by mining, work and capital could constitute important factors in the wealth of nations.

Today, financial capital is an important, even decisive, factor. At the same time, what has created the wealth of numerous high-technology companies today is often the collective intelligence of pioneering employees, whose only wages consist of stock options, worthless in themselves, but which can turn into veritable fortunes when their company, grown strong by success, becomes quoted on the Stock Exchange or sells out to the highest bidder. This form of capital is not visible. It is not invested in bricks and mortar or machines. As we have seen, the accounts of enterprises based on knowledge do not have much in common with those of traditional companies, whether in the industrial or service sectors. And yet it is a form of capital more essential than ever if a company is to develop within this new knowledge economy.

This form of capital, let us call it the capital of intelligence or intellectual capital, is gradually taking shape. The fact is that it has become harder to link the value of a company to its 'hard' assets alone, to machines and property. Looking at Stock Exchange transactions, or simply the prices quoted, it is easy to see that the real market value of a company is often not related to the value on paper of such tangible assets.

Between the hard assets and the value of the company, another added value inserts itself, that of *goodwill*. The accounts do not register it, except in a take-over situation, so in this sense this added value is written off for an indeterminate period of time. It is composed of the talents of the company's employees, the quality of its organization and its capacity to service and be loyal to its customers.

The three components of intelligence capital

In order to utilize intelligence capital, it is necessary in the first place to know and understand what constitutes it. The 'practitioners' of intelligence,[2] as it were, can be divided into three categories, corresponding to the three sources of energy outlined above.

Human capital, often referred to in the first instance, collects together all the talents of the employees of a company, their skills and their knowledge. This capital expresses itself in the daily life of the company; it renews itself over time and adapts to new situations as new knowledge replaces old and skills become more refined. Human capital is all the more valuable when the knowledge it mobilizes is irreplaceable in the eyes of the company's customers. Moreover, the increase in value of this capital is directly linked to the circulation of knowledge within the institution and the learning capacity of the individuals it comprises.

Structural capital, which is the second category of intellectual capital, is built up around the organization of the company, from the quality control system which lays down procedures to the systems controlling distribution, stocks and the handling of information, both soft and hard data. The structural capital allows the human capital to express itself. It is at the same time a framework and a tool, allowing individuals to increase and multiply their talents by organizing the ways in which they express themselves. Technological vigilance, 'learning teams' and other collective tools for the management of knowledge form part of the structural capital. At the same time, human capital and structural capital are of no value except when at the service of the customers, who form the third category of company capital.

Customer capital consists of the knowledge the company has of its customers, that is, the strength of the bonds that bind them. Customer capital is in the forefront when the loyalty of a company's customers is reinforced by the efforts made by the company to respect and enrich this relationship. The French are conversant with the concept of 'trading funds'. This is part of the customer capital, or rather the partial expression of this capital among the assets of the company. The customer capital is expressed in the trademark of the company, but at the same time it means conceiving of a product along with the customer, developing a relationship that can culminate in the creation of a common enterprise.

Looking at the evidence, we may see that these components are by no means new, but up to the present, like the tree, they have only been judged by their fruit. While admiring the fruit we have ended up forgetting the tree, and while entering the fruit on the credit side is one thing, it is still essential to develop the tree. And indeed, what is the good of priding oneself on a solid human capital if it is not able to save the company from going bankrupt? Or what is the good of developing an impressive structural capital with full ISO certification if this does not make the company competitive and innovative?

Intelligence capital – an asset or a liability?

Intelligence capital is measured by the value it produces on the asset side of the balance sheet, but it is managed on the liability side. It can be read off from the company assets – patents and contracts, trademarks, goodwill – but what we can see on the asset side is only the result of putting this capital to work. This distinction might seem overly subtle, but it is necessary. On the liability side, we find the company's creditors and shareholders, in other words, debts contracted or investments made that benefit the company. Investment in a new process may require several years, and the results may be seen in the accounts, for example in the form of a patent. Investing in a market, developing lasting relationships with future customers will one day lead to know-how and a steady stream of business backed up by trademarks or exclusive contracts.

ASSETS	LIABILITIES
Goodwill Databases Trademarks Patents	Intellectual capital
Buildings Product range Machines Stocks Customers Liquidity	Capital Debts Suppliers

It is therefore logical to add intelligence capital to the traditional kinds of capital that finance companies; customers and employees are to be taken as seriously as shareholders and suppliers. All these categories of people invest the intelligence capital they bring with them in the company. It may seem strange to mention customers and shareholders in the same breath, but these two groups together bring an added value to the company brand name. Brands do not belong exclusively to the company that promotes them. Coca-Cola found this out to their cost when in 1985 they replaced their traditional recipe with a 'light' version. The company was very soon forced to face the facts.

The customers felt they owned the product and did not like the new version, so the company had to reintroduce the classic version of Coca-Cola. Examples abound that reveal the shared ownership of a brand between a company and its customers. In short, when a company alters the image of its brand, it loses its customers. The same applies to human capital: a change of shareholders can be fatal to a company, since it risks gradually losing the energy which its employees put at the service of the company. This rich supply of energy, not quantified anywhere, but measured solely by past profits, can suddenly disappear into thin air, taking with it the company's brilliant results. Intelligence capital is a source of wealth for a company, to be placed on the liability side of the balance sheet along with the investments of shareholders and bank loans. This is not simply an accounting trick, but a major decision which can change the destiny of a company. Managing the three sources of energy of which it is composed is one of the new talents called for.

First source of energy: the customers

The first source of energy that powers intelligence capital, the customer, is the essential source of energy, although one of the most capricious. Generally speaking, companies that are preoccupied with their products, their know-how and their 'know-what' tend to ignore it. This source of energy only surfaces when human relations have become more important than the product, when what we have called 'knowing how to see' and 'knowing how to relate' (Chapter 2) are added to traditional 'know-how' and 'know-what'. Thus, customer capital puts these four kinds of knowledge on the company balance sheet. In addition, capitalizing on know-how and know-what form part of the basic skills of a company. We shall see later on that the challenge consists less in making use of them than in renewing them, but how are we to capitalize on the two other kinds of knowledge?

Capitalizing on 'knowing how to see'

Many companies do not 'see' their customers; they only see the transaction. Customers file past their counters or cash registers in anonymous succession. Transactions become progressively more productive; the company's know-how cannot be faulted, but it does not know how to 'see'. The last stage is to remove those people formerly in contact with the customers. What purpose do they serve, since there is nothing to see and a machine is a hundred times more efficient? The 'interactive' barriers at French railway stations are a good example of a transaction based on blind automation. Those companies that concentrate on the improvement of their know-how and their know-what also tend to reduce their sales networks. This means that there is no longer anyone to retrieve the information which would enable the company to understand how the customer thinks. In effect, they only meet the customer on the day when something goes wrong; and the encounter is often disastrous.

Others see so well that they end up replacing their suppliers. This would be the case of a large department store, which, by collecting information about its products and its customers at the checkout points, assumes such a powerful position vis-à-vis its suppliers that it can actually compete with them. 'Knowing how to see' is the secret of the success of Wal-Mart, the famous American network of retail stores, imitated today by retailers all over the world. The secret consists in a permanent 'seeing' process, which enables the company to see in real time the transactions taking place in its stores thanks to real-time systems of data collection linked by satellite. This makes it possible to manage stocks in the best possible way, as well as the logistics and the delivery of products to the places where customers need them.

Another example is that of Medco. This American company specialized in the direct delivery of medical prescriptions to patients, and ended up with such a dominant position in this field that it began to threaten the dominant position of the pharmaceutical laboratories. In 1993, Medco was bought up by Merck, not because of the company's distribution network, but because of its customer database, and its skills and experience in terms of customer contact. Here we find the three stages of added value explained above. Being able to 'see' the customer does not mean that one has physically to transport a product to the customer; mastery of the chain of virtual added value which links the product to the customer is often a trump card far more important than managing the 'blind' logistics of delivering the product. In this sense, capitalizing on 'knowing how to see' means using the modern techniques of *geomarketing*, which allow a company to draw up a precise map of its market. Making use of sophisticated software, a technique for the extraction of data can also enable a company to foresee the requirements of a customer segment, using a cross-analysis of all sorts of raw data to identify it.

Capitalizing on 'knowing how to relate'

Capitalizing on 'knowing how to relate' means moving from the simple transaction that is common to all forms of trade, to a more open form of exchange. The second level of 'relating' is what we call the 'product solution', and consists in adapting a product to the specific needs of a customer, who describes in more or less precise terms the product or service required. At this stage, we are still talking about the production process. The third stage, which we call the 'consultant solution', means that the supplier, rather than proposing the adaptation of a existing product, enters into the process at an earlier stage and works out what product is required based on the needs expressed by the customer. The final stage of 'knowing how to relate' is that of partnership. In this case, the customer might lay out in detail some function which a previous product had attempted to fulfil, leaving it to the supplier to devise some means of assuring this function, either alone or in some kind of joint venture. Whenever you cross from one stage to the next, and are the only ones to do so, you remove yourself from the sphere of direct competition; in this way, those involved experience an increase in quality and security.

An example of this is the Bien Joué company, founded some years ago by Jean-Luc Colonna d'Istria, whose success is based on a very simple formula: the company sells children's toys by mail order, and chooses the products to put in its catalogue by holding regular meetings with a panel of parents. Gradually, the products themselves take second place to the common concern to educate and entertain children.

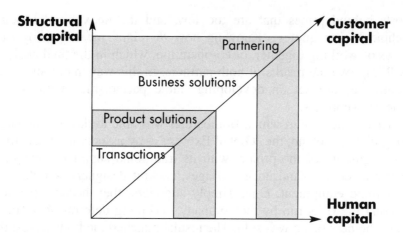

Source: from Hubert Saint-Onge/CIBC

Another example is that of Costco, one of the most profitable of American retail companies. One could hardly call its formula for success original: a club which customers join for about $40 a year. No, the secret lies elsewhere, in the company's ability to interact with its customers. The company operates with a 12% profit margin, while its competitors are looking for more than 20%,[3] and yet the turnover at its stores is double theirs. The loyalty of its some 15 million customers is such that the number of customers returning to its stores is in the region of 97%! Why should this be so? Simply because the company helps them to save money. The narrow profit margin of the retail outlets forces them to reduce their general costs to a minimum, while clearly indicating to the customer that their supplier is not simply growing rich at their expense. For its part, by only selling to loyal and reputable customers, the company reduces the risk of customers being in arrears, and minimizes losses due to theft.

Finally, the company uses the same techniques of interaction and exchange with regard to its suppliers; 'supplier capital' is symmetrical with 'customer capital'. From the point of view of its suppliers, every company is customer capital, and exploiting this capital means developing 'knowing how to see' and 'knowing how to relate'. Moving with them from transaction to partnership will allow us to enrich the value of our portfolio. In particular, 'knowing how to see' means seeing the supplier behind the price quote – identifying the hidden costs behind prices that are too low, and the unexpected benefits behind higher quotes. 'Knowing how to relate' means discovering ways of working together, of co-operation, which in the final analysis will improve the results of both partners. In this way, more and more companies are set on developing stable partnerships with certain selected suppliers.

This is the way in which Bombardier was able to develop its latest long-distance plane, the 'Global Express' – by associating itself from the beginning of the project with its traditional suppliers: manufacturers of engines and undercarriages, cockpit designers, suppliers of electronic equipment. Once simply suppliers, they became partners sharing the risks run by the company, accepting deferral of payment until the new plane was sold. The results matched the high stakes: the 'Global Express' flies faster than its competitors and has a wider operating range.

Another example is that of the Smart car.

> In order to produce its mini car as cheaply as possible, MCC, a subsidiary of Mercedes, set out to share all aspects of production. Preliminary studies were carried out with a group of eleven suppliers, renamed 'partners'. Seven of them established themselves fair and square on the factory site, where they were given good positions at the four corners of a site formed like a plus sign, or cross, if you like. MCC is 'only' responsible for the assembly of the various models, for the final quality check and for administering cars in stock... The advantages of the system are evident: research costs are shared as well as investments and the risks involved.[4]

Second source of energy: people

Human capital. This is a source of energy often quoted and often misused. 'People are the only source of wealth' – this famous phrase of Jean Bodin has opened many a discussion that has ended up by concluding, inversely, that it is difficult to speak of human capital without reservations. People are indeed a source of wealth for many companies, while for others they are a millstone from which they try to free themselves. These discussions reveal how difficult it is to 'manage' human capital. In the first place, it is obvious that human intelligence cannot be worked on like wood or metal. Second, a company is a 'reproduction machine', whether we are speaking of a product or a service. In this connection, computers can do more than human intelligence, more quickly and more surely. Intelligence is rather an inventive machine, often rebellious and sometimes unpredictable.

In order to utilize human intelligence, we have to recognize that the traditional form of organization, designed for simple reproduction without imagination or modification, is not suited to the 'management' of human capital. Therefore, we have to find another form of organization, better adapted to the task. This new form will first and foremost take account of the fact that the intelligence of the company employees is of no value unless the company knows how to use it to advantage. The company will have to convince its employees to place their imagination at the service of a common vision. Moreover, the company has to respect intelligence at work by guaranteeing the workings of intelligence certain basic freedoms. Finally, because human capital is not owned by the company, its loyalty has to be won, both in relation to the work done and the results achieved.

Vision: the richness of ideas, the value of knowledge

To bring the human intelligences at its disposal in tune with the company's overall project – this is beyond doubt the major organizational challenge. Human capital has become essential because the wealth of ideas and the value of knowledge have become a decisive competitive advantage, which the company must be able to benefit from. What point is there in collecting together people of high intelligence if they produce nothing good for the company? What is the point in accumulating knowledge and intelligence if the customers do not value what they 'produce', because there is no evident innovation or significant difference? How can we put the knowledge of each individual at the service of our customers, and make everyone motivated to acquire new areas of knowledge that can enrich the company's products in the future?

The time when the company was the primary, and indeed only, locus of our careers has passed. Today, the majority of us are more closely attached to our professions than to our companies. My company interests me if I can earn a living there and develop my talents, which are the sole guarantee of my future 'employability'. We are motivated both by the result and by the means of achieving it, so the company must be seen as the place where we exercise our talents. At the same time, this vision – both the result to be attained and the way we work to attain it – has to be shared by all. If we insist too much on one aspect, the result, we will end up forgetting that the process is what enriches our intelligence.

The fact is, we have to put all our cards on the table at the outset. People do not belong to their companies. True, as we shall see later on, our talents are not of equal value as regards the customer: some of us are replaceable, others possess talents so rare that a company will surround them with the utmost attention. Having said this, let us remember the importance of any weak link in the complex chain that creates the company's product range. Putting all our cards on the table means sharing information; it is on the basis of this that each person constructs his or her vision, and will know what to expect from the collective enterprise.

Process: the three freedoms

Financial capital needs rules in order to produce results, and the same applies to human capital. It calls for certain basic freedoms, namely, those of intelligence which we described in detail above. First, the freedom of time, which does not confuse the time spent in occupation with that of preoccupation; second, the freedom of space, which links intelligences from one end of the world to the other; and third, the freedom of exchange, which demands the inspiring diversity of dialogue and the time to pursue it. These processes are already well known. To ignore them is to call in question the very motor that drives the company within this new knowledge economy.

Attitudes: direct access

We have to put a careful watch on our human capital, making sure that its efficacy is not reduced to nothing by attitudes, by corporate or individual behaviour that in the end will annihilate innovation, the only product that can be sold on the market of knowledge.

First of all, we have to guarantee *people the right to act*. This is a basic principle. What is the point of mobilizing human capital if it is not able to express itself? Direct access to action, without intermediaries, gives people the freedom and the ability to take initiatives. We have all experienced seminars or meetings where ideas explode like

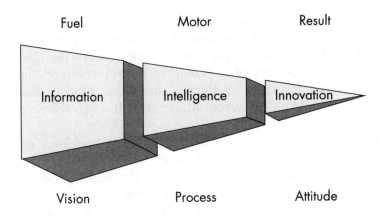

fireworks, and wild proposals abound. We have also seen these good ideas woefully abandoned because the rigidity of the organization precludes immediate action. With regard to France, a country where written laws abound, it is important to emphasize that companies are often hesitant to practise what they are always criticizing the bureaucrats for not doing – experimenting! The right to experiment is part of what we have called direct access to action. Guaranteeing this right also means removing unnecessary intermediaries; intermediary hierarchies, for example, remnants of the past rather than positive choices, often represent obsolete 'transaction costs'. At the same time, as we shall see in the next chapter, we must not 'throw out the baby with the bath water'; we must identify and reallocate certain functions that they perform and which are not obsolete.

Guaranteeing the right to act also means giving people the right to make mistakes, which forms part of the obligation to take initiatives and be innovative. If you acknowledge this, you have to find the right words to suit the occasion, like the tennis player who rather than shouting 'Missed!' when her opponent's topspin backhand plops limply into the net, cries encouragingly 'Well tried!'

The second 'right' that has to be protected, all the more so because it is the most abused, is clearly that of *direct access to information*. At the risk of being repetitive, we have to reiterate that intelligence becomes immobilized without the information that fuels it, and innovation becomes impossible. We have seen that people hide or filter information for thousands of reasons, and we know that if information is handed out in neat parcels (one might almost say 'formatted') most of its value in terms of the exchange and enrichment of ideas is lost. Direct access to information should be the rule rather than the exception. By controlling information, one reduces the intellectual sharpness and curiosity of the company's employees and dulls their critical senses. Inversely, intellectual sharpness, curiosity and a critical sense are developed when information flows freely. So why be afraid of it?

The third right to be accorded human capital is *direct access to results*. A banker who loans out capital is rewarded in the form of interest, a shareholder in the form of dividends. But how is human capital to be remunerated? True, people earn their salaries, but if we look at Bombardier and Smart with their partnerships and the stock options offered by high-technology enterprises, what steps are being planned by company leaders who wish to manage the human capital of their company in the best possible way?

Third source of energy: organization

Organization is the indispensable framework used to transform the knowledge and skills of individuals into company performance. Organization allows us to guide the chain of physical value associated with products and services, and the quality of it determines how well we will be able to integrate new stages of added value. In the broad sense of the term, organization is a mixture of acquired knowledge and skills, databases, forms of dialogue and procedures, and as opposed to customers and personnel, organization capital really belongs to the company shareholders. They have to manage it with care. Hubert Saint-Onge, one of those who has promoted the idea of intelligence capital, has modified the concept of structural capital by dividing it into three parts: production capital, organization capital and innovation capital. The process produces knowledge, the productivity of the organization continually improves and innovation produces new ways of working that are even more effective and economic.

Production capital

This is the most evident kind of structural capital. It consists of a collection of programs, procedures and digital data, as well as a body of knowledge and know-how assimilated by the people in the company. Whether digital or learned, this knowledge and data and these processes maintain and improve the day-to-day production of the company.

For several years now, capital has been going through numerous transformations. At the height of the industrial era, considerations of quantity and productivity were applied to the production process. The productivity of intelligence capital was low, automation was rudimentary, and most work procedures were manual. As competition intensified, customers made increasing demands on the quality of products and services, and then the speed of service became a major plus factor. Finally, as the last manifestation of the effects of competition, customer service became more individualized. At this point, productive intellectual capital took off: *soft* became more important than *hard*, and a wide variety of tools based on intelligence came into daily use in production: sophisticated programs for managing stores, complex production line control systems, digital telephone systems, automatic sorting, the ability to follow the progress of express parcels by satellite and so on. Today, productive intelligence capital allows a company to combine the highest quality with the lowest costs and to deliver products as quickly and as near to the customer as possible. Thanks to this, the performance of companies is not the result of a miracle, but of the common or garden use of this capital of know-how which has been accumulated and programmed.

ISO certification becomes part of this production capital as long as it is seen as a tool of intelligence. However, too many companies regard certification as a chore or a fad. Instead of using ISO as a tool in the service of their intellectual capital, they turn it into a heavy, external apparatus, which weighs down the company and slows it down. All too often customers of these companies are told: 'We're sorry, we can't deliver immediately, we have to follow the ISO procedures!'

In terms of production capital, it is also important to make a wise choice of tools for the transmission of knowledge and to make intelligence increase and multiply. Again we emphasize that these tools must increase the intelligence of the company, not limit it, as badly suited information systems all too often do. Finally, production capital involves a constant effort to maintain the relevance of that knowledge and those skills that are the basis of the day-to-day efficiency of the company.

The existence and the importance of production capital in a company can be seen from the void that is left if it breaks down. The breakdown of a sophisticated telephone exchange makes customer contact a nightmare; if your Intranet server goes dead, then your electronic letter-box is empty, leaving you deaf and blind. Nor is the future all that certain. Some companies, numbed by the fear of the year 2000, awaited with uncertainty the coming of the new century; others, unaware of the problem, were facing sudden death. Finally, all of them survived!

Organization capital

If the company is a vessel, its organization capital is the pilot, guiding all daily activities. It organizes meetings, writes memoranda, devises strategies, sales policy and personnel policy. It moves information and know-how, and spreads the skills required to feed the company's chain of value. In fact, it is this capital that structures the various resources of the enterprise in order to transform them into action. It allows one to see things before others do, and to react more quickly. Making use of one's organizational capital means setting up a tightly woven but lightweight structure which will enable the company to see, to foresee, to act, to judge, to innovate – in short, to know what to do, how to be and how to become.

In order to be effective, organization capital must be directed at the customer. This is not always the case. If it is badly designed or badly used it weighs down the company, wasting the energy of the personnel on pedantic checks and controls, pointless meetings and long-winded procedures. The point is to remove everything that is a waste of energy, like the well-known *mudas* practised in Japan. These *mudas* are akin to the once popular *tamagotchi* gadgets. For the benefit of those who might be reading these lines when the craze has disappeared and the term itself perhaps forgotten, a *tamagotchi* is a little plastic box about the size of a keyholder containing a virtual animal controlled by a simple program which endows it with the same kind of 'behaviour' as a domestic animal. The owner of the *tamagotchi*, often a child, has to make sure that its 'pet' eats, sleeps and keeps itself clean... a range of useless activities in which the owner becomes enthusiastically involved. In the case of a company, activities comparable to *mudas* and *tamagotchi* sometimes replace the customer and end up by devouring the energy so painstakingly accumulated by the organization capital, only to be uselessly frittered away.

One could say that the organization capital is really piloting the company when it helps company employees to analyse reality together. However, the further one rises within the organization, the more distant reality becomes. The highest positions are also those furthest removed from the customer, the products, the daily tasks of the company, and from all those who wrestle all the time with reality out in the field.

What actual means are at your disposal in your company to enable people to interpret reality in common? There are always meetings, of course, the panacea of large and imposing organizations, but they are held so frequently that in the end they only gather those who have the time to come, and not those who have the relevant information. These latter often cannot attend a meeting because they are too busy grappling with that reality which those gathered for the meeting, powerless to act, are attempting to interpret from a distance. Still, if reality is to be interpreted in common, people have to meet, and better use could be made of the tools available today for virtual meetings, from telephone meetings to video conferencing, plus of course simple fax or e-mail messages. Virtual meetings are effective because they put into effect the four rules of networking: the meeting has a purpose; the people taking part are relevant to the matter in hand; they are interactive for a real exchange of information, opinions and visions relating to reality; and, finally, the interaction is simple, which in the virtual world is always possible when the techniques have been mastered.

In effect, the tools available today enable us to analyse and direct reality through the flow of information. It is still normal to arrange meetings the sole purpose of which is to exchange data which could just as easily be accessed directly from a computer or received automatically by e-mail. Anyone could make a list within their own company of meetings which could have been avoided by making the information accessible on-line to all. It is difficult to develop organization capital in companies where information is still a sacred image, an inert object only shared out parsimoniously.

Organization capital, then, should enable us to construct ways of seeing, of foreseeing, and of projecting the company corporately into the future. It means making rules to outline a strategy and identify objectives; it means defining and preparing a plan of action, putting it into effect, and then following, monitoring and evaluating it. Now, all companies have their rules, but they do not necessarily constitute true organization capital. All too often, projections of the future have not been constructed with the support of the combined energy of the company, and therefore lack realism or any real content. Instead, charts are majestically presented with rows of imposing figures, all designed to sell 'happiness on the bottom line'.

Finally, if organization capital is to be developed, people have to know how to learn together. Machines cannot improve themselves, but people can learn. One of the levers that can be used to raise this capital is the establishment of a learning system which places the new knowledge acquired by people at the service of the company. A unique way of capturing, ordering and capitalizing on this knowledge is to give pride of place to teamwork and other tools of collective learning. A disparate collection of brilliant individuals will never make up collective know-how. Learning is the way in which the third form of structural capital, innovation capital, will develop.

Innovation capital

This is what gives us the resources to act differently, to renew ourselves and to renew our company. It enables us to initiate, manage and carry through existing projects. Patents, trademarks and all the things invented by the company are the products of this capital.

In order to manage your innovation capital you have to work out specific rules for being inventive. In this way, 3M's ability to innovate has made it universally admired: it has 8,300 researchers distributed around the world in many laboratories, linked by their professional skills, their technology and their freedom to work independently of the company decision-makers. Redundancy is one of the key concepts with regard to innovation capital.

It is also a question of learning those rules of co-operation which alone allow for the kind of interaction where differences meet and enrich each other. To see a handshake as a trial of strength rather than an alliance is a powerful test of the innovative capacity of a company.

The innovation capital of a company can be measured by looking for the part played by new products in the company's turnover and in its profits. Many companies have taken this step, showing 25% of the turnover as made up by products and services less than four years old. In this way, one can renew one's product range before one's competitors do so!

The four laws of intelligence capital

At the end of this list, new demands appear over the horizon. The essential forms of capital, our resources, have changed. We know how to manage the earth, and manage money, but what about intelligence? New laws apply here.

Basics. The first law collects the three sources of energy. Together, they comprise the intelligence capital of the company. As the evidence shows, they cannot develop independently of each other. Rather, the development of the one completes and enriches the other. Without organization, without intelligent production, without innovation, and without people to initiate and maintain these energies, it is hard to attract and keep even the least important customer. Inversely, when the main purpose of the organization is to control people's behaviour rather than to spread 'the spirit of service, of teamwork and of progress', organization capital becomes an encumbrance, and useless as far as the customer is concerned. On the other hand, human capital and customer capital reinforce each other when, as was the case with artisans in former times, producer and customer know each other, accept each other and respect each other. The producer draws new motivation from the satisfaction of his customer, and looking critically at the service he has provided finds new ways of improving it. Organization and customer mutually support each other when each learns from the other and learns from this exchange how to set up a type of organization truly oriented towards the customer.

Ownership. The second law separates the three sources of energy. The point is that although the company may be the sole owner of its structural capital, its organization, its procedures and its strategic secrets, it is only the co-owner of its personnel and of its customers. The company has to admit this and apply this knowledge to its activities. Companies who enter into conflict with their employees, their customers, or maybe their suppliers, may perhaps achieve some immediate gain, but by doing so they preclude all future co-operation, which is the source of their wealth.

Value. The third law makes distinctions. Assessing the wealth of a company means putting a price on its intelligence capital. The apparent value of its structural capital may be impressive, but all that counts is how well its strategic competence is developed. A sophisticated organization bereft of 'company spirit' would be a handicap. Customer capital may appear manifold, but it is of no value if the company is blind and cannot see the customer behind the transactions. Finally, a collection of brilliant individuals is worth less in terms of human capital than the fruitful conjunction of complementary talents. In the final analysis, and this point is not new, the company's three sources of energy are only worth the value the customer assigns to them.

Management. The fourth law remains to be invented. Emphasizing one source of energy rather than another presents a risk. Organizing a company around its structural capital means going back to seeing customers and personnel as mere tools, merely technical constraints on the company. In the same way, organizing a company exclusively with a view to its shareholders, financial capital and profits comes down to seeing customers and employees as costs to be reduced. Finally, organizing a company around its employees will bring it into decline, heading off course along the road to self-satisfaction. What then, do we really have to organize a company around its customers? This idea is in vogue at the moment, but the customer, if he becomes the company's final objective, does not cover innovative responses on the part of the company; if you follow the customer, you cut yourself off from imagining the service which he has not dreamed of yet, but which he will be delighted to discover is something he cannot do without.

So, in order to organize the three sources of energy, we have to recognize that they are anthropomorphic, that they have a human shape. Human capital and customer capital are made of flesh and blood, whereas structural capital, from process to innovation, is only an abstraction from the intelligence of those people who make up the company. In the light of this, making the best use of the three energies that fuel intelligence is undoubtedly a question of organizing the company around people, whether customers, or those who produce added value. This presupposes abandoning the time-honoured model for company organization based on the mechanical metaphor of Taylor's theory. It was necessary to take a detour around this metaphor in the past, but today it is a blind alley. If we construct a company that resembles its customers and those who work there, rather than its products, we will have a company based on relationships, a learning institution in perpetual change.

Action, relationships, learning – these are the three challenges of the hypertext company.

Notes

1. René Char, 'Feuillet d'Hypnos', *Œuvres complètes*, Paris, La Pléiade, Gallimard, 1995.
2. This chapter owes much to two books with similar titles: Thomas A. Stewart, *Intellectual Capital,* New York, Currency Doubleday, 1997; Leif Edvinsson and Michael Malone, *Intellectual Capital*, New York, Harper Business, 1997.
3. www.costco.com
4. *Libération*, 21 October 1997.

How to Change a Wheel Without Stopping the Car

ACTION

You have to imagine Sisyphus happy.

Albert Camus[1]

First a whirling cloud, then a long black scarf trailing lazily above the rooftops, suddenly the flock of starlings transforms itself into a sharp tongue of lightning, striking down to fill the trees of the square with raucous squawking. Companies would like to resemble these flocks of birds. Impeccably lined up or in seething disorder, companies carry out the most unforeseeable manoeuvres in perfect order; they can move in an instant from apparent repose to lightning action.

As customers, we expect the company to be in tune with our desires, whether foreseeable or not. We expect it to master all the moves, from the most simple to the most complex. We expect it to satisfy our fascination with what is new and our affection for what is unchanging, to provide the solid excellence of the 'déjà vu' and the heavenly surprise of novelty and progress. 'Surprise me, but don't change my habitual ways.' When a company disappoints us we quickly become unfaithful, as Mercedes learned to its cost with the flawed launch of its new Class A car. In the same way, Intel admitted that its new Pentium II had certain weaknesses, and the Apple company, despite the devotion of its customers, has lost important sectors of the market... and yet, companies that react quickly end up by winning back the goodwill momentarily lost.

A company must master both speed and slowness with the same degree of expertise. As customers, we love speed: 'Hurry up, I don't have the time to wait.' A simple click of the mouse, a single telephone call, one short look at the sales assistant, and we require an immediate

138

response; we demand the most elaborate service, the newest product, here and now, without delay. At the same time, we like things to move slowly: we expect people to listen patiently as we fumble to express our needs; we like long explanations, a detailed description of the way a product works, or simply the pleasure of being recognized, of being given a helping hand, of passing the time of day.

As employees of a company we are very much like our customers. We love the security of a settled employment contract, of a familiar situation, while at the same time we want to cheat boredom and be innovative in our daily work. We would like to speed up routine tasks while taking the time to learn and to find new ways of doing things. As far as our shareholders are concerned, they savour with delight the regular influx of dividends, but are nonetheless open to new adventures that bear fruit. They become impatient when progress is too slow, but are prepared to 'spend time on time' when the development of the company is moving too fast for them.

The company resembles us when it assembles us to require our services, and when it hastens to put itself at our service. The company learns how to be foreseeable and yet full of surprises, to be both fast and slow, to master both routine and innovation, to be indifferent and passionately involved. It learns how to combine in a talented way the know-how applied every day with 'knowing how to change' everyday things.

Know-how and 'knowing how to change'

'The manager of the 90s is someone who can change the tyres while the car's still moving.'[2] In fact, this definition of the job of a leader, attributed to Jack Welch, the President of General Electric, applies to all company employees, leaders or not.

The point is that our everyday work has radically changed. On the one hand, we have to be beyond reproach in providing the service which our customer has the right to expect of us. In fact, we have no choice, as the competition is ready to pounce on our smallest mistakes. On the other hand, we have at the same time to be ready to adapt and change the service we offer, to make swift improvements to it, or even radically transform it.

Our professional work no longer consists of programmed activities, evolving in a linear, predictable manner along the lines of the Taylor model. It is being reshaped at every moment by the need to adapt to new and increasingly diverse demands, and in this uncertain climate our profession cannot survive unless it can offer an immediate and appropriate response to them. This in turn supposes that the person offering the service has been delegated total freedom of action – of competence, authority and knowledge. The hypertext company organizes its daily work around this double manoeuvre of 'doing the job' and 'changing the job'. It knows how to combine speed and caution, routine and change, how to 'do the job' fully and completely, and how to 'change the job' gently, discreetly and yet effectively.

In order to win the race, we have to be able to 'do the job properly' all the time, and 'to change the wheel properly', that is, constantly to check and revise the service from which you make a living without stopping at the side of the road to do this, or 'pulling into the pits'. This is a difficult exercise, and no imaginary challenge. In fact, our professional work these days is shot through with these two kinds of 'knowing how', which are inextricably linked: everyday know-how, competent and detailed; and 'knowing how to change' – the ability to anticipate change, to assess its consequences and to apply it without a hitch to the everyday workings of the company. We have to be able to reproduce the old and invent the new, at the same time, and in one movement. Sales are continuing even while we are working!

We are far removed from the Taylor model of an organization, the efficiency of which was based on the precise reproduction down to the last detail – ad infinitum and in imposing quantities – of carefully measured actions and pre-defined procedures. This was the price of productivity. Today, on the contrary, efficiency is based on the quality and the relevance of the decisions taken (when to produce, what to produce?), and the ability to set in motion a new process adapted to the needs of the customer.

In order to evolve, many companies have been forced to reorganize; others have remained faithful to the old model and have disappeared. However, there are still many companies who are caught in the crossfire, and are wondering how they should change their way of operating. They find that their present tight, transparent and efficient way of running their company is not allowing them to follow the whims of their customers. Should it therefore be replaced? How are they to evolve? How is permanent change to be incorporated into the very organization of the company?

Here are several replies to these questions, illustrated from practice.

Know-how

The immediate pressure on us in real time leaves no time for orders and instructions. It is essential that each employee who has to face the customer be able to make the appropriate response. This is what we could call the first dimension of know-how, and it means that in the daily work of the company each person can act without recourse to the hierarchical structure; that each person has direct access to action, without intermediaries; that the information required for action is available without restrictions or useless passwords; that the tools are distributed to all who work at ground level.

This also implies that there is a clear set of ground rules, as autonomy is not possible unless the organization is transparent and the rules explicit. Moreover, formulating these rules calls for time, discipline and a capacity for dialogue.

Finally, if the company is to be at its best when it moves into action, all the 'know-hows' have to be mobilized and distributed, they have to be, and remain, relevant, and they must be collectively available rather than just the prerogative of a few. What is the point of having the power to act if the skills are lacking?

Knowing how to change

'Changing the wheel without stopping the car' means organizing the company so as to make each person the initiator of change by incorporating 'knowing how to change' into the structure of organization itself.

'Knowing how to change' means recognizing that people have the talent to do the job and the talent to change. Managers often lock themselves inside their ivory towers by maintaining that their employees are good enough at their jobs, but do not know how to change. The fact is, though, that we all possess this talent, as recent years have shown, but it can only be developed if management can see it and will allow it to unfold.

'Knowing how to change' means locating a puncture before it occurs. Within a company, this can be done in the first place by identifying and opening certain *black boxes*. A 'black box' is a procedure, a task, even a whole line of work, the application of which is essential to the company, but which no one as yet has really mastered.

KNOW-HOW	KNOWING HOW TO CHANGE
Relevant The knowledge and the tools to do the job	**Identification** of 'black boxes' **Implementation** of teams able to resolve tensions **Contracts relating to objectives** with a system of measurement
Explicit Transparency of the network and the rules of the game, which is a condition of multiple meanings and of close-knit co-operation	**Agenda** encompassing all the actions required by change **Rhythm** written into all interaction within the company **Follow-up and renewal** by steering committees embedded in the other co-ordinating and decision-making structures of the company
Autonomous Knowledge must be able to be applied without reference to the structure	

The difficulty in opening these boxes is not least connected to the fact that people tend to denounce other people's black boxes, and not their own. They are afraid of losing their own independence, which is locked away behind a veil of obscurity, and indeed by the relative efficiency of this particular piece of know-how, the contours and principles of which are jealously kept undefined. For this reason, no one can be sure any more that the hidden knowledge contained in these black boxes is still relevant and useful. It could, for example, be a computer program which did a good job when it was installed, but which has become obsolete in the course of time. Everyone suspects this, but no one dare touch it, and the company continues, more or less, to advance. Those who use the program have ended up with certain procedures, often clandestine, to interpret the data, and people come to consult them as in former times seekers went to the oracle at Delphi. But now the company's much-trumpeted victories have turned into ignominious defeats; it is time to lance the abscess and open the black box. For example, one might find that in a company which regularly has too many products in store that the 'producers' criticize the unrealistic predictions of the 'sellers', who in turn are surprised by long manufacturing delays for which they have to 'cover'.

To identify, open and then perhaps remove these black boxes is a painful step, but necessary. The naked reality exposes the obsolescence of the corporate system to the eyes of all. Many of us have experienced these moments of tension when everyone is looking around for a scapegoat, and in general the person who has played the role of Delphic oracle becomes the chosen victim. However, this is rarely the best solution, as the black box has usually spread its gangrene throughout the whole organization. An accusation against one of us quickly turns back on the accuser. Therefore it is essential to gather a group composed of all those who have been involved in the activities that are under suspicion, so that none of them can exonerate himself from the responsibility. At the same time, they have to agree only to address the problem before them on the table rather than attacking the people sitting around it.

Companies are becoming more and more complex, and black boxes are increasingly numerous. However, choosing to eliminate them often proves difficult because they interact one with the other. In order to put some power behind any planned change, one has to gather all the planned changes into one agenda, which will establish a rhythm for all the meetings and activities of the company and provide an 'arrears list' which can be checked off.

This common agenda is only possible if the organization of the company can demonstrate that it has built know-how and 'knowing how to change' as priorities into its basic structure. This process often begins with traditional steering committees that collect the various people involved in a project, but once the meetings have been held, the traditional hierarchy tends to reassert itself. Projects unravel, and routine rules again. In order to avoid this pitfall, some companies include in their organization a management committee for change. This is what DHL-France did when faced with the need for swift and reliable deliveries, and for a global service delivering close to the customer. In fact, their management of change covers 'the three key levers of change: information technology, total quality, and the service of the customer'.[3] Other companies, although as yet not many, have gone even further, replacing traditional boards of management by steering committees, making change not just an attribute of the company, but its very substance. All those who are running projects are members of these steering committees, irrespective of their place in the hierarchy. This type of organization not only unites all those directly responsible for change, it also allows them to enter into a dialogue which enables them to see the relative importance of the projects and their interpenetration. And indeed why should the search for better quality not have an impact on stock management, or be itself influenced by efforts to cut costs?

So, when the list of things required to 'know how to do the job', and 'know how to change' is complete, one sees the way in which the hypertext company operates. But how are these qualities to be written into the very foundations of the organization? At this point we must once more have recourse to the birds.

The company flying like a bird

Craig Reynolds is a special effects expert at Silicon Studio. In order to create flocks of birds or swarms of bats, as in the film, *Batman Returns*, he uses a simulation program to create captivating effects. He only uses three basic formulas, which applied to the flight of each of the virtual birds allows him to create an animated image which comes very close to the flight of living birds, or bats.[4] When applied to a company, these formulas suggest three principles of organization.

Stand alone. Separation

The first principle is that of separation. Each bird flies on its own wings, without interfering with its neighbour. Each keeps its eyes on the line of flight and looks towards the same horizon. Applied to companies, this would mean that each person, each organization, should stand alone and move forward without treading on each other's toes.

Standing alone is a new talent. In traditional forms of organization we had become used to being part of the system. If the system changed, we changed; if the system was immobile we all marked time together, becoming obsolete together and finally disappearing. Standing alone is a talent which has to be cultivated. Companies that suddenly decide to organize themselves as a network often discover this to their cost. They pass on responsibility to their employees, but are completely bowled over when these people begin to act on their own initiative. They delegate vast projects to others, only to discover too late that those who manage them are not sufficiently autonomous. At this point there tend to be long, contrite speeches about the lack of responsibility and difficulty of delegating responsibility.

Standing alone means being autonomous. But, in the strict sense, an autonomous person is 'governed by his own laws'. To be autonomous in a company is not to be independent, but implies that one accepts and masters the constant flow back and forth between individual rules and company rules, respecting both.

This double movement has given rise to the concept of *empowerment*: on the one hand this means showing confidence in people by delegating authority, and on the other hand that these people are able to accept this delegation, to be autonomous.

Empowerment

Empowerment is a word much in vogue, although if it should fall from grace the concept behind it will survive. (In French it might perhaps be an advantage to replace it with a term which was still used in the 18th century, but which has fallen into oblivion. This is the term *emport*,[5] which originally meant 'carrying weight, having an influence on someone or something', but which is used derivatively today to express 'carrying capacity', or 'payload', for example the payload of a plane.)

Empowerment is a reality of the company today: the tools of communication are within the reach of all, and provide those who previously merely obeyed orders with more power and autonomy. Each can take the shortest route, as fast and as far as possible, without any intermediary.

By giving power to the most modest link in the chain, *empowerment* gives new shape and vigour to the principle of subsidiarity, which was defined several centuries ago as the basis of social organization. It is a simple principle: never pass on to a higher level in the hierarchy a decision which can be taken at a lower level. Back in 1982, the Centre for Young Managers (in French, CJD) suggested in its 'Good Management Charter' that decisions should be taken at the lowest level of a company, by what they called 'ascending delega- tion'. This would make each person responsible for his own actions. *Empowerment*, ascending delegation, the principle of subsidiarity, shared authority – all this presupposes that the company is a true network in which power is distributed to all without discrimination.

But the irony of history is that at a time when the need for delega- tion has become pressing if we are to face, or even anticipate, an increasingly competitive and changing reality, many leaders take over the reins, subjecting their employees to rigid controls and reporting procedures, thus limiting their room for manoeuvre while resolutely calling on them to take initiatives. It is not always easy to give greater power to the most humble of one's subjects. Some are afraid of placing confidence in others, some are afraid of losing their power by passing on information. Others again think that their employees will quite simply not be able to assume the responsibilities delegated to them. Because the company needs lightness and rigour, flexibility and security, the contradiction between the need for delegation and the fear of doing is more than ever very real today. What can be done to get out of this trap?

Monkeys and Teflon

Hubert is the production manager of a medium-sized company, which has been working for a long time without foremen. Visitors are aston- ished: 'how can you manage the 60 people in this workshop?' His answer is courteous and unassuming; 'it would indeed be impossible if they were not autonomous; in fact, I only discuss important matters with them or serious mechanical problems. I meet them individually every six months to take stock of the situation.'

Many managers and leaders are bowed down under the weight of their daily work. Their subordinates are like children, constantly badgering them, asking for permission to do this, to do that. They are respected for their mother hen role; one finds them comforting those beset with problems and reprimanding those who cannot solve them alone. All these cases add to their collection of 'monkeys'.

'Monkeys' is a well-known metaphor[6] for the absence of autonomy. Monkeys are generally born in the corridors and of random encoun- ters: 'Pierre, I have a problem', confides the foreman to the site director. 'Tell me about it', answers the director. The foreman details his problem, a 'splendid monkey' rich in technical details and human errors, touching many fields that the site director knows well. He does not hesitate: 'I'll take care of your problem', he says. The foreman goes away, feeling quite unjustifiably contrite, but relieved of his monkey. As for the site director, he saunters proudly on, a new monkey on his shoulder. Everyone ends up seeing this and knowing that Pierre, the site director, loves monkeys, so they all entrust their problems to him. Pierre, festooned with monkeys, feels irreplaceable.

At the opposite end of the scale, other leaders, better informed or quite simply 'animal haters', have developed a 'management by Teflon' technique,[7] a practice which consists in giving up any kind of driving role in the organization, in the name of decentralization. Reports, problems, glide off them as if they were coated with Teflon; they never become involved. Physical dispersion of the company tends to encourage this kind of 'furtive management', which is no more conducive to the development of autonomy than the breeding of monkeys.

Rights and duties of the autonomous person – the 'author'

It has to be said that empowerment and autonomy – which come in somewhere between monkeys and Teflon – are 'bilateral'. A leader must understand that exerting his authority means 'making his subordinates into authors'. This is his most important role. Any obstacle to their autonomy is a loss of energy and effectiveness. He has paid for their talent, then let them express it! The organization is only a support, not a hindrance. If each person is to become an 'author', then the network of exchanges within the company must be fully functioning. Autonomy is not a solitary act, it is a permanent grid of actions which make the added value of the company. To put this simple precept into practice, a manager has to carefully organize his time, with the intention of using it to make others into 'authors' rather than putting himself in their place!

As for the person to whom authority is delegated, he must have the talent to exert it, a real *author's talent*. To be an author means controlling the know-how which contributes to the creation of the value of the company; it means building up, developing and using one's own goodwill; it means having the hammer and the nail and knowing how to use them. But it also means resisting the temptation to become jealously locked up within this recently acquired autonomy.

Vincent Lenhardt[8] divides this *author's talent* into four stages: the first, that of the doormat, is the inability to take initiatives. This is the stage of dependence, of the 'yes-man', and those who do not want to delegate often parade it as an example to show the inefficiency of delegation. The second stage, known as that of the 'hedgehog', or that of contra-dependency, is that of the teenager who is discovering his personality by saying 'no' all the time. Then follows the stage of the 'rascal', that period of savage independence, where each person sets out to experience the world alone and 'without a safety net'. The last stage, which he calls 'unison', rounds off the training of autonomy. Here, one learns that it is essential to stand alone and to fly on one's own wings, but that the company involves collective action, and all those involved are interdependent. No one flies all alone.

To work together. Alignment

Alignment is the second principle. Each bird must co-ordinate its movements with those it is flying with. Within a company, the second key of the action is to know how to work together. This second condition is quite as obvious, and quite as difficult as the first. How to get autonomous people to move forward together? How will they catch the right moment, find the right direction?

How will they choose the right partner to ensure service of the customer? The question does not arise within traditional structures. Here, the process is pre-established, immutable. So much the worse for those who do not conform to it, be they customers or employees. Recently, the Taylor chain of command has been 'spring-cleaned' by the 'invention' of internal customers. This step has certain merits, in that it directs all those involved in the company towards the customer. Its principal defect is that by creating internal customers along the chain of value it preserves the sequential and rigid nature of the Taylor model, which is insensitive to change, and restive in the face of uncertainty. Those who supply part of the product might think that they have satisfied the internal customer, while leaving the true customer stranded at the edge of the road.

To work together, each one standing alone, means acquiring the habit of working 'with' others rather than 'for' another. It means putting one's store of goodwill at the service of the customer, through the company. To work together is not to work in sequence, but in a network. The tools of today enable the customer or his supplier to be in direct contact, at any moment, from anywhere. This is also true inside the company. To work together in a network presupposes giving up the rites of sequential work and using all the resources of the network. Peter M. is the director of a group of companies distributed throughout the world. He has formed the habit of regarding each of them as a separate domicile, on the basis of the familiar principle that a network does not have a centre. Moreover, the meetings in which he participates do not only gather those who are physically present, but all the possible virtual participants, in real time or asynchronous time. Thus, at a meeting in Singapore, a new investment project is being discussed, but certain important technical details are lacking. Guillermo B., the director of the Mexican factory, knows them. At one time, the meeting would have stopped at this point, but today Peter calls Guillermo to a video conference, and in a few minutes information about the missing elements is exchanged. Thus, the decision is made, using the combined intelligences of the group. When the physical and virtual circle cannot be closed because someone or something is not available, the exchange continues on the Internet and the meeting becomes fully electronic. For those who really want to work together, the time has passed when those who were absent were wrong. The role of the leader is no longer to mitigate the absence of his employees by installing a new monkey on his shoulder. On the contrary, it means making sure, by all the means now available, that all the force of the company is gathered around the making of the important decisions. It also means accepting, without ulterior motives, that the power lies with the people sitting around the real or virtual table.

The rules of the game

To work together we have to know the rules of the game and know how to play it. The basic rule is mediation. But the delegation of responsibility which builds autonomy often overshoots the target because the corridors of the organization are not marked or are badly known. Generally, these corridors are dark and cluttered. There is a plethora of rules. In order to manage increasing complexity, some organizations have developed a whole forest of procedures and standards which define everything, from the essential to the peripheral. Knowing the rules is a special kind of know-how, and applying them becomes a science, or rather something like divination. Those who have neither know-how nor particular competence are reduced to following the rules scrupulously when they know them, or having nothing to do when, as is often the case, they do not know how to interpret them. The instinct to conform takes precedence over the temptation to run risks. The company becomes a sophisticated and motionless system of administration.

When writing the rules of the game, one has at the same time to imagine the action to be taken according to the situation and to admit that one cannot foresee everything. The merit of certification procedures is undoubtedly that they enable one to write some scenarios. The rules of the game are at the same time messages and blank pages on which each one can write his own code of behaviour, for although the rules of the game are necessary, they cannot take account of all possible situations. To admit 'incompleteness' is not a weakness of the organization. As we have seen above, writing rules which say less and less about 'how' and more about 'why' is one of the components of working in network.

Laying down rules comes down to determining the direction of the action to be taken, and respecting them simply means allowing this action to take place. This is not always the case. Julie is three years old. Her mother is teaching her the rules of the house: 'In the kitchen you must not go near the oven or the hotplate, you could burn yourself badly.' Julie, who is mischievous, approaches the forbidden oven and puts out her hand. 'Julie!', shouts her mother, half-serious, half-amused. The game begins. Once, twice, Julie tries to transgress the rule, but after the third time, her mother does not laugh any more and stops her with a sharp command. Julie starts to cry, quite put out. When the rule is important, there is no place either for indulgence or negligence. This is also the case in a company. There is some rule of the game which has never been applied. Suddenly, the leader decides to demonstrate his authority and suddenly brings the rule into force. Those who are the victims of his sudden overzealous behaviour fail to understand. The leader is not the master of the laws, he is only the guarantor.

Two talents for working together

To work together also calls for new talents. No action is solitary. The author must know to integrate his creation into the common task. A mere juxtaposition of intelligent and talented craftsmen is not enough. Today, this *talent for integration* has become essential, as companies are spread more and more widely in space. Each person must perceive his role and his place in a chain of value which has become less and less physical. Our fellow workers are often virtual and silent: a file sent by e-mail, parts which arrive from the other end of the world and which have to be integrated into a machine designed elsewhere and assembled here. These transitory bonds die and are then reconstituted; each time we have to find the tone, the shade, the degree of familiarity which characterized them. How are we to integrate things when we are permanently zapping from one link to another, between our multiple suppliers, partners, subcontractors, co-contractors? A new talent is definitely called for.

The second talent connected with 'working together' is the *talent of relating*. It is not just a question of mastering English, the Internet and other tools of globalization. The talent of relating is not a kind of technical know-how, but initially a talent of empathy, the 'capacity to be identified with others, to feel what they feel'. The network, as we have seen, needs to know the identity of the participants and the first essential step is to know how, with a few words or gestures, to create, externalize and construct the group, perhaps virtual, within which the exchange will take place. The second step is to establish a dialogue, to mingle one's own knowledge with the knowledge of others and to create a common added value together.

Mutual enrichment. Cohesion

The third principle is cohesion. Each bird must follow the average direction which emerges from the overall movement. Cohesion implies co-operation, which makes mutual growth possible. The strength of an organization is at least the sum of the combined work of its members, but it is also more than the sum of its assembled talents, and for this to happen these talents have to mutually enrich each other.

It is a difficult exercise in a traditional organization, which knows how to spread orders and rules, but not knowledge or know-how. Mutual enrichment implies a double movement. To enrich the others, it is initially necessary to have something to give; you have to know how to fly alone before you can be a resource for others. Daily know-how is only effective if it is relevant; each must possess the minimum knowledge which will enable him to remain autonomous and act autonomously. This is a platitude, but it is often forgotten. How can you enrich others when your last training course was ten years ago? How can you enrich others when you no longer have the time nor the desire to learn more yourself? You need, therefore, to want to be a resource for others, and this means knowing how to give before you receive. The Indian wrestling test described in Chapter 3 offers a quick measure of the degree of co-operation which exists in a company. This double movement relates to the content as much as to the direction of co-operation. The force and the talent of the others create the desire to emulate. The strength with which they fly in a particular direction reinforces in us the idea of going there together.

Co-operation calls for two talents. The first, the *talent of direction*, is the same as insight. It is not a question of exchanging or building anything. Each act of each employee of the company must be able, as in a hologram, to be congruent with the others. Insight means at the same time knowing how to open up and how to close in on oneself; to know what direction to take. The second *talent*, that of *content*, means knowing how to build bridges across to other knowledge, to other partners, in order to enrich the co-operative game. The 'bridge maker' calls new meetings to renew the learning process, and brings forward the best practices for comparison, seeking outside the company those new elements which will raise new questions, those which will give a sense of direction to the learning process, and then to the action itself.

The hypertext hierarchy[9]

The network advances. Its rules take shape. The hypertext hierarchy is built up little by little, just like the links one establishes when surfing the Internet.

The term 'hypertext' was suggested in 1965 by Ted Nelson to describe documents that revealed the non-linear structure of ideas. Applied to a library of files, the hypertext technique consists in chaining these files together by a non-sequential fabric of connections. These links thus enable the user to navigate among widely varied subjects without keeping an account of the order in which they were arranged. The links can be established both by the authors of the hypertext documents as well as by the user, depending on the subject of the document. Consequently, the hypertext, mainly in its interactive form where the choices are dictated by the user, tends to offer a working and learning environment as close as possible to the human way of thinking.[10]

To make a purchase in a traditional way, there is only one way to go: take the road that leads to the store, then go to the floor and the counter which have the product you want to buy, and queue up to pay for it. The hierarchy of these choices involves you in a logic which you can only leave by going out the way you came in. This is the market place in physical space. On the Internet market place, you have multiple points of entry. You can seek the product directly, choosing the cities or the streets where it is sold; you can compare prices, pay for the product by a click of your mouse, without queuing up, and have it delivered without leaving your desk.

The traditional hierarchy took the road of physical added value, that of the market place. The hypertext hierarchy follows the virtual links of the market space. A private individual looking to invest some money goes to see his banker. If the product offered does not suit him, he will have to beat a courteous retreat and go to another bank. Today, thanks to his favourite search engine on the Internet, he can find and leaf through the best investment sites, analyse their performance by consulting the files of specialized magazines, and, via a safe-payment module, buy the investment plan that gives the best results.

In this way, perhaps, you will buy your next computer via the Internet. Rather than being content with the computer available in your store, which will be out of date in at least six months, you will thus have the advantage of the most recent components, as well as the configuration, the computer power, the peripherals and the software most adapted to your needs. Your order will instantaneously set in motion a chain of value, from the purchase of the components to the delivery of the finished computer. Behind the screen, you will have called upon a particular company, undoubtedly several. The Internet shop window from which you chose your computer is undoubtedly only one specialized server involved in this rapid and convenient way of taking an order. The technician who then takes care of the assembly of your computer will himself make the choice, in real time, of the fastest suppliers of the least expensive components. As for the fast delivery service which will bring your computer to you, it was consulted, along with its competitors, at the moment when you finished placing your order.

The companies in which we work are getting more and more to look like networks. The hypertext hierarchy is not yet the norm, but one can see its outline behind the autonomous teams, the short lines of communication, the increasingly differentiated methods of working, the externalization of certain activities...

These companies are becoming less and less transparent in terms of the traditional criteria of organization. 'What has become of the foremen we used to have?'; 'Who really runs this company?'; 'No one gives orders any more, it's quite confusing!' How are we to move from the traditional hierarchy to the hypertext hierarchy? Many think it is enough to reduce the number of levels in the hierarchy, so that the pyramid would have its base in the network, but how can hierarchical principles based on a physical entity, the pyramid, be applied to a virtual network?

There was a certain logic behind the pyramid hierarchy, and before transforming it we have to understand it, so that when we change it the essential principles will remain. Moving from a traditional structure to a flat structure presupposes the suppression of hierarchical levels, but in removing them what is really being removed? How far can this exercise be taken? In addition, the functions exercised by the hierarchy which one wants to remove, and which are necessary in a network, will have to be reassigned. What functions are these, and how is it to be done?

The classical hierarchy was founded on three principles of cohesion: 'all the forces which act on the members of a group so that they will remain in the group and thus resist the forces of disintegration'.

Socio-affective cohesion goes back to the attraction that the group has for its members, with the idea that the greater the attraction, the more the group will be cohesive. The socio-affective factors lie in the interpersonal relations which bind the members together, in the attraction of a common goal and in the status attached to membership of the group...

Socio-operational or functional *cohesion* depends on the organizational methods with which the groups are equipped, on the communication networks, on the nature of the task, the size, the distribution and interrelationship of roles, the style of leadership, and finally on the degree of adjustment of resources in relation to the activities of the companies...

Normative cohesion refers to the thoughts, beliefs and attitudes produced in common in order to provide the group with a framework of reference for deciding what is desirable...

These three types of cohesion are interdependent. The concept of cohesion thus seems essential to understanding the structural and functional aspects of groups.[11]

These three dimensions are not simply academic constructions. It is enough to look at the life of a manager of a small company to find these three dimensions at work. As the founder of the company he knows its work processes by heart (the operational dimension), and often puts in a hand 'at the lathe' himself. It is also he who sets the standards. Finally – or in the first place – it is he who creates the relationships and sets the pace, creating the *affectio societatis* without which there is no company, but only an institution.

Gathering these three dimensions in his own person, if his company grows, he will often delegate them in bulk, such as a gang leader would to his right-hand man. The operational dimension will be divided along the major technical functions of the company (technical, commercial, financial...); this is what appears in the flow charts. The two other dimensions – relationships and standards – will generally be linked and will become what we have agreed to call the 'culture' of the company, defined and distributed according to the seniority of the people and the jobs they do. When the company grows, or quite simply when it must face changes which call into question the practices of the group, each of the three dimensions starts to go its own way. The process changes, becomes more and more complex; groups multiply and are spatially scattered; certain functions are externalized. Standards are not diluted in diversity, but human relations change with the increasing disparity of the jobs done. The company gradually drifts off course. Cohesion begins to fray at the edges.

The manager decides at this point to take over the reins again himself. If he follows the traditional way, he will build a pyramid with many floors, supposedly suited to controlling the complexity of the new building. The three dimensions are ignored, and confusion has in fact settled in; the necessary initiative and delegation are often blocked by the inability to go beyond the culture and change the relationships.

It is important, in the process of turning the company into a network, not to throw out the baby (the three principles) with the bath water. It is essential to recover the three dimensions and the associated roles which they imply in the structure of the network; they could be distributed between several people, provided that none of them lacks any of them. The operational competence could perhaps be shared between the operators and some experts who are called to their assistance. The standards, and the authority that rewards or sanctions, will be able to handle many people. As for the regulating and facilitating functions, they will be ensured by a team leader, whose only mandate will be to facilitate the work of the team and its relations with the company environment. With the proviso that none of the three dimensions is forgotten, one could imagine many alternatives, depending on the situations that arise: thus, an expert could be given the mandate, or the responsibility, of leading an activity.

In this way we can do away with the traditional foreman who holds the three functions: authority, expertise and relationships. One can replace him by an expert who will intervene at the request of the teams; to facilitate relationships, an organizer selected from each team will ensure internal links and the relationship with other parts of the company. As a result, the management of the factory will be able to concentrate on its essential task: to define the direction of common action, to maintain and nourish the intelligence capital, and to allocate the resources necessary for success. This dissociation of functions is necessary, both to face the complexity of the situation companies find themselves in, and especially to allow for the development of new initiatives. Each person can refer to the group by calling upon the three functions as required: resort to an expert, the need for guidance or relationships with others, a need to know what the standards are.

More than ever before, the 'hypertext hierarchy' questions the traditional mode of cohesion assured by the classical hierarchy. Nonetheless, the basic principles remain.

- *The operational principle*: the customer did not have a choice of the way to reach the company, and the future was foreseeable. The top of the company could see it, the base followed, although it was not affectively involved. Today, information no longer descends from on high, it pops up at the click of a mouse. Those who face the customer have all the power. The operational hierarchy ignores traditional channels. The chain of value is built up starting from the choices made by the customer.

- *The relational principle*: because the customer followed a foreseeable route, the hierarchy held the monopoly on relationships; it determined both internal relations and external relations. Today, e-mails are unaware of etiquette and precedence. People meet online, although discussion groups need organizers who can get the process of exchange moving again.

- *The principle of authority and direction*. The hierarchy set the standards. The company was one and indivisible; the hierarchy gave orders, dictated the activities of the moment, the place and the direction. Today, everything occurs so quickly that it is necessary to make decisions closer to the customer: it is he who directs the usefulness and the direction of the company. It is not a question any more of knowing on whom one depends, but with whom one is working and why.

The flight of starlings circles and whirls in perfect unison. The hypertext company takes shape:

- *Separation*: each of the modules stands alone; it possesses and cultivates its own goodwill, which can be called upon at any moment, randomly. The hierarchical chain of command must accept the zigzag course imposed by the customer. Expertise enriches the company much closer to the action, in its daily activities and in the process of transformation.

- *Alignment*: between the intrusive management by rules which slows down the mobility of the unit, and the untrammelled autonomy which ends in chaos, we find the idea of alignment. Alignment is only possible if the rules which guide action are not complete, so as to make allowances for the diversity and complexity of situations. It reveals the common intention to work together, 'with' rather than 'for' somebody.

- *Co-operation*: authority bases its reputation on the interpretation of the rules, rather than on fastidious, even blind, respect for them. The hypertext hierarchy is an asymmetrical and multi-linked hierarchy, constantly reorganized. It must accept that the goal requires the hierarchy to be inverted; that internal discipline dictated from the top down must make room for the logic of the customer. All the actions of the company are tied together around the customer, and it is also here that dialogue is concentrated.

Notes

1. *Le Mythe de Sisyphe*, Paris, Folio essais, p. 168.
2. From *Control your Destiny or Someone Will*, p. 261 (paperback), New York, Tichy/Sherman, Harper Business, 1994.
3. *O1 Informatique*, 21 November 1997.
4. Anecdote quoted by Thomas Stewart, *Intellectual Capital,* New York, Currency Doubleday, 1997, p. 181.
5. One could coin the term 'empotence', which would be closest to the meaning, but too close to 'impotence' to be really symmetrical with it.
6. Bill Oncken, *Managing Management Time: Who's Got the Monkey*, Englewood Cliffs NJ, Prentice Hall, 1989.
7. Guy Pelletier, 'Les virgules du temps', *Expansion Management Review*, September 1995.
8. *Oser la confiance*, Bertrand Martin, Vincent Lenhardt and Bruno Jarosson, Paris, Insep Editions, 1996.
9. Expression taken from Philip Evans and Thomas Wurster, *Harvard Business Review*, September–October 1997.
10. *Encyclopédie® Microsoft®*, Encarta 1998.
11. Catherine Thomas, PhD in Management Theory at the University of Nice, defended her doctoral thesis on this subject in December 1997.

8 I Do Dialogue, and So Do You?

REGULATION

Listen to the silent man.

Japanese proverb

In the past, when you knew where you were going, you went there, in an orderly and quiet fashion. Today, when all futures are possible, silence has become dangerous. Dialogue is essential.

As customers, we demand it. We prefer the companies that can build up and nourish our choices. They can listen to us in silence, but they find the words which express our needs and the answers that satisfy them, without arrogance or undue insistence. We like the companies that listen to us without pestering us, that can recognize us or respect our anonymity. They share our passions, our enthusiasms, our uncertainties and our concerns.

Seen from the side of the company, dialogue is also essential. It is the invisible and permanent web of exchange and contact which links us together amid the tasks and aims of our daily work; we need dialogue to apply the rules, to understand their purpose, to expand them and adapt them to face new situations; we want to speak and be heard, to be respected as persons, to be able to intervene, to challenge. Finally, we know that listening to our customers, and being able to answer them is a difficult exercise, but richly rewarded in terms of loyalty and innovation.

The hypertext company is most at home with itself in the changing, unforeseeable and demanding relationship that dialogue calls for.

However, whether customer or producer, we are afraid of dialogue; it can shake our deepest convictions. We do not like confrontation, because it can call us into question. It sometimes happens that meeting someone changes our ways of seeing things, and kindles in us the desire to tread new paths that we would not have dared to take before.

Dialogue is necessary, but we prefer discussion. Dialogue is difficult, and we are often unaware of the techniques to be employed. However, dialogue is an engine which builds us up and moves us forward.

Dialogue is necessary

Dialogue is the framework for action. It enables us to exchange our images of the world, and to construct the rules which will enable us to live and make progress together. In the first place, it enables us to interpret reality together.

'The first responsibility of a leader is to define reality', wrote Max De Pree.[1] Today, this responsibility rests on all those who work for a company, because the reality facing the company is commensurate with the dimensions and changing face of the planet itself. It is, moreover, the counterpart of delegation and autonomy: we have to make sure all the time that everyone is marching in the same direction, and that one's ideas are understood; that in spite of the diversity of our markets or trades, we share a common reading of reality and the way we act upon it. Dialogue is initially a way of representing reality by confronting one's perceptions of it with those of others, but defining reality together presupposes that we talk about it together, equal to equal, that we practise and structure dialogue, the pursuit of truth. Dialogue also enables us to discover our areas of knowledge and ignorance, and thus it is at the source of all learning.

However, dialogue often frightens us. As leaders, we are afraid that it will call the management of the firm into question, and will lead to a clash between divergent visions of reality or of what kind of future is desirable. As employees, we are afraid that it will bring out our weaknesses. Dialogue presents a risk, and for this reason we often prefer discussion, where each person uses arguments as weapons to destroy the other's position, without assimilating it. If we agree to chair a meeting without prejudging the results, we are putting all those who attend the meeting on an equal footing, making them 'authors' of the common dialogue and of its conclusions. Many do not wish to run the risk of trusting people, but they end up as captains of a vessel where the crew is deaf and dumb, obedient but unresponsive, and insensitive to any change which the captain himself has not ordained.

However, dialogue is more than ever necessary. The hypertext company is permanently forging new relations, new links. Dialogue makes it possible to establish a common vision by reducing uncertainty, and it constructs the rules of the game. If we try to impose a rule without giving those affected by it the chance to discuss it and to adapt to it, we are courting rejection, incomprehension, revolt; the best answers are given to a question well put, and which only dialogue can give rise to. The company must innovate. By encouraging meetings and the exchange of differences, dialogue makes it possible to give birth to and exchange ideas, dreams and uncertainties.

To enter into a dialogue means recognizing that one needs the other. The 'single thought' is precisely the absence of dialogue, and in the context of a company it means being surrounded by yes-men. On the contrary, if we have sincere opponents, we give ourselves the chance to describe together a reality which each person will be able to feel involved in.

Dialogue is difficult

Too much accustomed to living the regulated life of the traditional hierarchical company, we have come to forget where and why dialogue takes place, as well as the techniques. For this reason we feel awkward when we sincerely want to move forward. Here are some techniques, borrowed from experience and put together with the support of experts, including Peter Senge[2] and Alain Gauthier.[3]

The first stage is to properly understand the difference between discussion and dialogue. If dialogue is the confrontation of two ways of thinking, it often becomes the closed room of discussion. The weapons are known: rhetoric and dialectic. The outcome of the combat is certain: the defeat of one of these ways of thinking.

Those familiar with dialectical techniques know how to choke their adversary by asphyxiating his reasoning, ideas or images. The famous *Dialogues of Socrates*, transcribed by Plato, do not account for the true nature of dialogue. From the very start of his dialogue, Socrates knows the outcome. The whole purpose of the encounter is to help the pupil 'give birth to' an answer. The starting technique is simple, and resembles the techniques used to neutralize the left brain presented earlier in this book. By assailing his interlocutor with fundamental questions, requiring him to state the difference between the beautiful, the good and the right, to define friendship or love, Socrates defeats his adversary's left brain. The dialogue so constructed has to lead to a dead end, an aporia ('doubt'), which is used as the prelude to a new teaching process. This dialogue technique of inducing doubt is often used: those assembled around the table intone their favourite refrain with its foreseeable ideology and rhetoric; the chairman, generally a director or top-flight manager, shows them the dead end towards which this dialogue of the deaf is leading them. Then, before the eyes of his confused colleagues, he pulls out of his hat the principle or miracle cure that will do the trick. The effect is spectacular, but there has been no dialogue.

A dialogue supposes two parties, both seekers. The basic rule of dialogue is to accept that the convictions of each are two legitimate positions, and that only a demanding and reciprocal enquiry can produce a result acceptable to both.

Entering into a dialogue, therefore, means in the first place expressing these convictions. The images of the world which confront each other can be very different, and it is vital to give each person the time and space to express them. At this stage, one notices that many people, undoubtedly afraid of being drawn out or discovered, remain withdrawn, but it is essential that they come out of hiding and relinquish the position of observer. In a dialogue, one has to accept that one is both observer and observed, questioner and questioned.

The next step is then to question the opposing point of view, to understand its tenets and boundaries, structure and direction. This is the second axis, that of exploration and interrogation. It is quite simply a matter of questioning the convictions of one's adversary, initially in a courteous and 'academic' way, although too much academic questioning can transform the dialogue into a simple interview. The other person's ideas have been perfectly presented, but there has been no dialogue. Television provides us with many examples of skilful discussions. The interviewer, or host, adopts a neutral position. The discussion swings between precise interview questions and inflammatory statements; when people are given a limited time to speak, nothing really happens. The listeners return home, strong in their unaltered convictions or their unrefuted questions.

In a dialogue, conviction and exploration (that is, exploratory questioning) are first opposed, then reinforce each other to produce a common result, a process which is sometimes chaotic. This fumbling conflict of ideas will produce a profitable dialogue only if certain very simple rules of the game are observed.

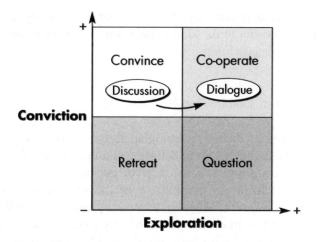

The four stages of dialogue

We all retain the nostalgia of these magic moments of true dialogue. One remembers the place, anonymous or unforgettable, but definitively associated with this moment. One remembers the sharp exchanges, the moments of doubt; and one relives the final moment of intoxication, when the members of the group, proud of their collective product, of an unexpected solution, separate with regret, dreaming of living through similar moments again, but already conscious of their scarcity. Conversely, we try, generally without success, to forget those meetings that have been less than fruitful. Noisy or quiet, elegant or brutal, they were filled with violent exchanges, with sledgehammer remarks and conclusions, with skilful duels and vibrant campaign speeches. Many meetings do not produce anything. Everyone complains openly about this, but are secretly delighted. The meeting ritual had been respected: a review of the situation, an exchange of viewpoints on the problem facing us. Often, a simple barter of words is enough, after which each person can leave the meeting serene in the knowledge that the surface of entrenched convictions and certitudes has hardly been scratched. The ritual has been observed, but the problem still remains in its entirety, as there was no dialogue at all.

To restore the chemistry which is at the basis of dialogue is a difficult exercise. In order to do so, it is necessary to progress through four stages in strict succession.

From invitation to deliberation

One cannot simply decree a dialogue, it has to be gradually introduced, and the first steps should not be ignored. First of all, there is the *invitation to dialogue*. This order of events is often forgotten by those who want to get to the marrow of the subject at once, but by doing so they prevent the slow but essential process of building up the group. The point is that dialogue can only exist if the group exists over and above the individuals involved. One has to play oneself down, and accept that one is at the same time observer and observed, speaker and listener. Once the scene has been set, the participants are entitled to a few introductory remarks to find their voices; this is the beginning of *conversation*, when each one turns to the other (which is, incidentally, the etymology of the verb 'to converse'). One is reminded of the African 'palaver' and its long introductory rites. The next stage, that of *deliberation*, is in fact a circular process to determine the nature of the problem which is to be the subject of the dialogue; the participants deliberate on the causes and nature of the problem as set forward. The principal actors are introduced. Strangely enough, one should be on one's guard if agreement is reached too quickly. If this is the case, there will not have been any dialogue, but the process of discussion will have been started.

Discussion or debate

This is the most critical stage on the road towards the dialogue, and consists of violent attacks and frustrated silences. The group hesitates. Each person is well aware that he could withdraw without all the fuss and bother of discussion. To discuss means listening to the opposing point of view patiently and courteously before joining in to present one's own arguments. If the participants agree to be influenced by the arguments of the others, the discussion can move patiently forward towards true dialogue. At this point, it is necessary that the participants explicitly and reciprocally accept that they can be influenced by the others. If not, then inertia or eagerness will turn the discussion into a debate. The dialecticians, the lovers of rhetoric and the virtuosos of the set language piece will throw themselves into a debate with all their hearts. The opposing camps clash. The listeners applaud each new salvo, each new encircling movement. The battle is a delight to the eye... but the outcome is piteous. After many sallies backwards and forwards across the field, the noise dies down and silence prevails. The dialectical attacks did not fool anybody; the spectators and the actors are tired of the spectacle. The meeting is over.

Discussion and dialogue

On the other hand, the meeting can take a different turn if the participants recognize the failure of the meeting and analyse the reasons why. In the first place there are objective reasons: if, for example, the causes of the problem were not properly analysed and shared. In this case, advancing towards dialogue will consist in building up a common understanding of the situation. Words that do not have the same meaning for all should be explained. Certain situations, obvious

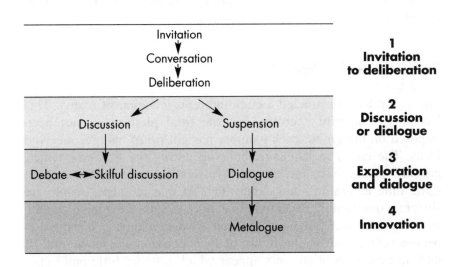

Source: after Peter Senge, *The Fifth Discipline Fieldbook*

to some, are unclear to others and have to be explained. Neither should one hesitate to explore those dead ends behind which the levers of true dialogue often hide, but which are taboo: what do we agree on? What do we disagree on? Then there are the subjective reasons, which arise from the game being played by the participants themselves. Meetings fail when the participants (and this is the only point on which they tacitly agree) have decided at the bottom of their hearts to emerge from the meeting unchanged. It is essential that each person is conscious of his own intentions: his hesitations, his will to agree to be influenced by the others. Each will have to analyse the way he evolves as the meeting proceeds, and agree to be observed, without complacency. Nor is it a question of disavowing one's convictions, but of finding a balance between special pleading and a sincere questioning of the different points of view.

No wonder people begin to feel weak at the knees. There is the impact of people's convictions. The edifice has first to be undermined, and then reconstructed amid a myriad questions. One hears the avenging angels passing overhead. Doubt settles in; nobody is sure of anything any more. The group is suspended in mid-air; it is faced with more questions than answers, more uncertainties than solutions, and this is a source of worry. But at least these questions are shared, and this is a source of pride. It is time to set the dialogue in motion.

Exploration and dialogue

The group has constructed a common representation of reality. This has been a painful exercise, but the final picture has not been imposed on the group; each member has got rid of his preconceived ideas. The common language, built up during the first two stages, provides a solid basis for the real investigation to start. This is at the same time enthralling and exhausting. At one moment, people are sincerely questioning the convictions of others, the next moment they get cold feet and fall back on their own certainties. When some people venture out to the limits of their convictions, to the end of their questions, new answers appear which little by little build up a new reality.

Innovation and metalogue

This is the last stage. A collective image has emerged which has nothing in common with the narrow convictions of the beginning; a common language is being established, based on common agreement. Each person appropriates this new reality to himself, mourning for his lost convictions and the comfort which they brought. If one of the participants is having difficulties in advancing, the others bear him up, investigate his idea and try to accommodate it. It is enthralling to see the participants, brought together by the effort required, become united in body and spirit, building sentences and ideas together. The rhythm has changed. The representation of this new reality is no longer outside the group; the group itself is this new reality. Even so, the dialogue makes no sense unless the end product materializes. This is the 'metalogue', the product of the common effort; what it produces is a work of art, a step forward, an action, a programme, a concept which will transform the company little by little. Today it is perhaps its product or its leading service, but whatever it is, each person will remember for a long time that dialogue can transform a dead end into a royal road. Having said this, it is not enough to know the stages of the dialogue for it to produce its results. It is also necessary to know to insert it into the everyday life of the company.

Organizing dialogues in daily life

Inserting dialogue into the everyday life of the company – dialogue between the employees, and with the company's customers and partners – calls for time, space and certain signs.

Time

Dialogue requires time. This time appears to many as a waste of time. This is particularly the case in traditional companies where everyone waits until the leader makes a decision. The leader is not willing to give this up, and very often decides first and consults later. This foible is well known, but it persists for all that.

Dedicating time to dialogue means not to be afraid of silence and breaks in the meeting. Silence is often a moment necessary for the assimilation of the idea which has just been put forward. It is no use trying to break it by adding more words. You have to let the images and ideas work their way down into the minds of each person present. Breaks should also be accepted: we find it quite normal at a congress or conference that a committee spends some time reflecting on the ideas presented at plenary meetings. Why cannot we do this in our companies?

This was the lesson learned by a certain manager during the take-over of another company. In front of the assembled personnel, he presented the reasons which had made him choose to integrate this company into his group, and then explained the main axes of his strategy. Having finished his presentation of the company, he asked his listeners if they had any questions. Several moments of complete silence followed. He tried again. Then one member rose: 'This is not the way we usually do things', he said. 'Oh, I see, well what is your usual procedure?' 'We take a break for a few minutes and then put our questions afterwards.' The break is agreed, and people gather in small groups to discuss. Ten minutes later, the meeting begins again. Questions are fired from all sides, precise and incisive. Each one had used the pause to 'validate' his own questions and share them with his neighbours, or to check that the question which he wanted to raise was not completely stupid. Everyone, even the shy or timid, had found a spokesman. The ensuing debate was satisfying and comprehensive, and the dialogue was finally set in motion.

Space

Dialogue needs space. The space of a room, a corridor, an open forum. Too many companies, utilitarian in their thinking, have removed any empty space, thus excluding places for dialogue. To save on space required for dialogue is to accept that all spaces can be diverted to this use. Office spaces become general-purpose rooms. Real dialogues only take place on the margins of the company, between people leaning on bars in pubs, or chatting in the workshop changing rooms. Setting aside space for dialogue means neutralizing spaces which are consecrated to this purpose.

André had been looking for this round table for a long time. He had had enough of erudite tactical ploys; from one works council to another, the rectangular table in the conference room had transformed dialogue into a constant juggling for position. Today, a shiny new round table, around which more than 20 people can sit down comfortably, puts everyone on an equal footing. Dialogue may not be easy, but it has become less difficult.

Toronto, 1997. The 3,000 employees of Northern Telecom leave the glass towers of the company headquarters for a disused factory on the outskirts of the town. The vertical framework has become horizontal. No more high-rise floors, but a ground-floor space covering the equivalent of 50 floors. The architects organize this space into districts intersected by boulevards and streets, with meeting points designed to favour improbable encounters. The 'inhabitants' of each district have each shaped their own space.

Signs

The handshake exchanged on the lawns of the White House between Yasser Arafat and Yitzhak Rabin is etched into all our memories, the organ swell of a tough but profitable dialogue. It is necessary to show what the dialogue has produced. The simple minutes of a meeting must account for the opposing points of view. If we do not gloss over the differences which were resolved in the final consensus, we demonstrate that we have changed, and learned, together. Thus, the signs of dialogue become a powerful motor of future action.

Dialogue is a motor[4]

Above all, dialogue is the motor that powers action, and it is through dialogue that we discover the desire to act or not to act. Dialogue shows us a new reality or a new goal, and gives us the desire to learn. It gets us moving.

'Movement' is the root and literal sense of the term 'motivation'. *Motivus* is derived from the Latin verb *movere* (to move) which gives us 'motor' and 'motivation', 'mobile' and 'mobilization'. As soon as we begin to speak about motivation, each of us can use his own approach from there on. In the first place, there are the theories of needs, propounded by Maslow and Herzberg. The former treats our various needs on a hierarchical basis, and this theory has been much commented on. In practice, apart from the obvious application, such as in the saying 'empty bellies have no ears', few of us use this theory. On the other hand, that of Herzberg is worth remembering: it says, in substance, that only content motivates… but that the context can demotivate; it is essential to worry about working conditions, for example, but an unsuitable physical framework can be demotivating. Conversely, an idyllic setting will not be enough to motivate people. They need other reasons. At this point, other theories can come to the rescue. This is the true of the cognitive theories which, rather than dwelling too long on the content, the 'why', make a lot of room for the process, the 'how', and for the movement of life itself. Last, 'regulation' theories maintain that to give oneself a goal, or to have goal laid down for one by somebody one respects or admires is also motivating. All these theories, without explicitly saying so, have adopted dialogue – as motive, motor or movement – as their centre of gravity.

Motive

In order to act, we need a motive. A hero harangues the crowd in a film: some are his faithful supporters, others bitterly oppose him, and they all present their arguments. The discussion becomes heated, words and gestures fly, now and then there will be a pregnant silence. At the end of the scene, eyes shining, all step out as one man behind the hero. In the reality which is the company, things are less simple. How are we to start on the first stage of a long voyage? Each person will have to find, through dialogue, the motivation for starting at all. To do this, the dialogue will have to be set up, consisting of questions put and answers given, convictions honoured and curiosity satisfied, and providing the reasons for action. The dialogue must enable certain questions to be answered, questions of which Vroom has constructed a theory of motivation. Without answers, that is, without dialogue, nothing will happen. Can I see this through to the end? This, in the language of Vroom, is *expectation*, the hope that the action will be successful. What will it cost me? This is *instrumentality*, the price to be paid to reach the result. Last, or perhaps initially, does the voyage which we will undertake represent an interest? Does its utility have any value for me? This is the concept of *valency* (in its non-scientific meaning of 'energy' or 'vigour'), that is, the value which I put on the voyage, subjective certainly, but the only thing that counts in relation to the effort that will have to be made.

Movement

Once the motive has been found, the stage is set for action. In this phase, too, dialogue is still essential, as the interest attached by others to my action will be important. This is where theories of content can be brought in, based on the famous Hawthorne experiment. The experiment took place between 1927 and 1929, in a factory belonging to Western Electric in Hawthorne, near Chicago.[5] To increase output, it was decided to rationalize working conditions, but to no effect. Finally, however, one particular measure produced results. The intensity of the lighting was varied from workshop to workshop, from the brightest possible down to the weakest level (0.3 lux), that of ordinary moonlight. Productivity increased by 25%, paradoxically in the least well-lit workshops. The 'researchers' ended up by concluding that productivity gains were not due to the improved working conditions, but rather to a change in the relations between the management and the workers, and consequently between the workers themselves. Dialogue is relationships – this is, as we have seen, an important dimension of the hierarchical principle. The hypertext company must seek to establish moments of dialogue, even of mere chat, which can reinforce the motives for action and give it new sense and direction. Meeting and speaking with one's neighbours gives people the energy to continue their onward flight.

Motor

The action is completed. Now is the time for debriefing, for assessment and analysis, a phase which people too often try to avoid. However, it is essential to know how one arrived at the appointed goal, and to state this clearly. It is essential to remember the mistakes, the successes, the fears and joys of acting together. This is the moment for each person to acknowledge, identify and name his share in the common task, to assess the influence he has had. Dialogue allows what each individual has contributed to be generally known, and gives people the will to start over again – it has become a real driving force.

At the end of an eventful year, Pierre, the director of a medium-sized company, was preparing the general meeting to assess the year's work. He recalled that the same meeting the previous year had not been an unqualified success: the columns of figures, the details of investments, the markets won after a bitter struggle, even the take-overs of other companies – all this had left people cold, and the problem had not been the quality of the overheads. People did indeed feel involved, but 'could not find themselves in the figures'. He decided to ask the members of the works committee to prepare the meeting. They arranged a number of investigations, surveys and interviews, but in effect only one question was being asked: 'what was the most important development for you personally?' The answers were presented in front of the assembled company by the people who had been interviewed themselves: the new showers, the microwave oven in the cafeteria, and the new computer network which saved production operatives a lot of time produced a much more successful meeting than the histograms and pie charts of the previous year. However, it was the last chart that raised thunderous applause: it presented portraits in colour, according to sex and date of birth, the detail of the babies born in the course of the year. Here was a major change which no statement of figures could account for: confidence in the future, symbolized by the newborn children of the company employees!

Notes

1. *Leadership is an Art*, New York, Dell Books 1990.
2. Peter Senge, *The Fifth Discipline Fieldbook*, New York, Doubleday, 1994.
3. Alain Gauthier worked with Peter Senge to translate *The Fifth Discipline* into French.
4. Yves Rajaud, 'La motivation', *Progrès du Management*, October 1994.
5. Elton Mayo, *The Human Problems of an Industrial Civilization*, 1928, reprinted as a paperback by Ayer, New York, 1977.

9

The Robin, the Titmouse and the Bottle of Milk

LEARNING

Learning means growing day by day.

Lao-Tseu[1]

Volvo car factory in Ghent

The visitor on a hurried visit to this spectacular factory, from which 150,000 vehicles emerge every year, is often only left with the memory of the ceaseless and gracious ballet of the robots that weld, assemble and stick parts together, or of the waltz of the intelligent transporters which move the vehicles in silence from one assembly point to another. Many do not notice the educational display boards scattered around the factory. The purpose of these miniature exhibition stands is to allow the teams to exchange their good ideas, their know-how, or their solutions. Drawings, photographs and diagrams posted there allow for the fast and thorough transmission of knowledge; moreover, diagrams in the shape of a flower, where each team is a petal, make it possible to measure the dissemination and adoption of these practices throughout the whole factory. In this way, productivity has doubled in six years. The factory in Ghent has several times won the prestigious TPM (Total Productive Maintenance) prize.

In a factory where the robots predominate, the work done by men is essential, for only men can make progress. The celebrated German mathematician, John von Neumann, has summarized this as follows: 'the difference between man and machine, is that the latter is degraded as soon as it starts to function, while man improves with working!'[2] Technology makes knowledge into a fundamental energy of the company, whether it is a question of the knowledge that one

173

transforms into a program, a robot or a machine, or of the knowledge that each person carries within himself. All this knowledge combined enriches the intelligence capital of the company.

The stakes

The hypertext company reproduces and invents through action. Through dialogue it builds visions and finds new ways. But what am I to do when the image changes and obliges me to change occupation? Action and the dialogue are only of any value by virtue of the content that is exchanged, that is, the quality of the know-how put at the service of our customers. In the era of the craftsman, to learn meant looking at, then copying the actions of the master, but today's knowledge is to be read in people's brains rather than in their hands. How are we to transmit a thought, an idea, a line of reasoning? Moreover, knowledge is used up so quickly that there are no longer either masters or pupils, but alternately the one or the other.

The hypertext company is both a formative and a learning institution. It is formative in order to enrich the daily work; it is a learning institution in order to acquire the new knowledge for which the customer is waiting. In order to make a company really formative, its intelligence capital has to be made to bear fruit, and existing know-how has to be diffused throughout the company. In the same way, a learning company is one that can locate and acquire the knowledge required in the future. Learning is the third dimension of the hypertext company.

Three things are at stake in the knowledge game. First, it is a question of diffusing existing knowledge to ensure the excellence of the daily work. This implies making knowledge a quality tool, by locating those who harbour it, and deploying them to best advantage in the organization, in order to improve the structural capital of the company. Second, it will be necessary to identify or uncover the knowledge which will constitute the professional skills of the future, the competence which the customer expects to find in the company. Finally, it will be necessary to learn, individually and collectively, how to acquire and transmit the knowledge of today as well as that of tomorrow: learning and teaching on the one hand, and on the other managing and organizing both knowledge and learning.

Apart from the 'technical' investments required to remain in the race, we know that a company can only be effective if its employees use to the full all available skills, both in themselves and around them. It cannot progress unless they can develop their skills and put them at the service of the customer.

If it is difficult to plan, decide on and implement a material investment (a machine, a building, a computer, additional memory storage, a new hard disk, updating software and so on), it is even more difficult to decree and then obtain an increase in the knowledge and skills of the men and the women who make up the company.

Several obstacles present themselves along the way. In the case of the manager, there is the difficulty of identifying, beyond the knowledge and skills necessary today, those which will be essential in his company tomorrow; in the case of the employees, there is on the one hand the difficulty of understanding the nature and the necessity of, and the stakes involved in, this improvement, and on the other their own motivation to improve their skills. Finally, all are faced with the difficulty of finding and implementing practical, applicable and accessible methods of learning these new skills, whether individual or shared.

Here then, is a small treatise on how a company becomes a learning company, in three stages. First of all, we would identify in our companies the layers of present skills and the areas open to improvement; in the case of both managers and employees this means the management of knowledge. Second, we would propose practical methods of shared learning by drawing up a collective learning strategy. Last, because to learn is at the same time to teach and learn, we would study those essential tools and types of behaviour which make it possible to acquire, disseminate and renew our skills, and which distinguish learning companies from those which are merely formative. The examples and concepts presented here result mainly from work undertaken in 1996 within the CNPF commission, 'The Progress of Companies'. Manfred Mack, Max Boisot and Alain Gauthier have helped me define the few development tools presented here.

The management of knowledge

The learning company is *à la mode*, but before describing the process, we shall speak a little about content. What fields of knowledge are we talking about? Do they all have the same value? Who are the holders of the essential fields of knowledge? Are they at the top, at the bottom, or outside the company?

Identifying fields of knowledge

Some fields of knowledge are banal; others are not original, but can be competitive levers for the company which implements them. Finally, there are those rare fields of knowledge which are not found elsewhere and which make a company irreplaceable. They are also called 'key areas of competence'.

'Banal' know-how is the basic know-how required to enter the game: how to type a text, answer the telephone, send out an invoice... all essential types of know-how, but they do not make the company special.

'Lever' know-how is that which, by itself, is not very original. Having said that, however, when used properly in a company it substantially increases the value of its product range. In the sector to which a particular industrial company belonged, the traditional commercial practice was to present one's customers with an incomplete, quite repelling list of prices in black and white. Deciding to use the techniques of mail-order sales, the company sent its thousands of customers and subscribers an annual price catalogue in colour instead, which was both attractive and interactive. This know-how was the lever which placed the company in a leading position. Another example is a classified advertisements company which has developed by using the Internet, while its competitors, the daily newspapers, continue to print and distribute tons of paper.

'Particular' know-how is that which distinguishes the company from others. It builds up the company's market identity insofar as this competence becomes identified with the name of the company. It takes the form of established patents or irreplaceable trademarks; it is a 'key competence' because it has a unique value for the customer that its competitors do not possess, and which can be placed at the disposal of the customer in a way that is reliable, continuous and constantly renewed. It is knowledge on which the future of the company can be built. It can be a body of various types of technology and knowledge. For Swatch, for example, it is at the same time a low-price manufacturing process and a way of communicating; for

Coca-Cola, it means mastery of the message and the key elements of the packaging process.

In order to manage its store of knowledge, any company could make an inventory of its skills along these three axes. An inventory of 'banal' know-how may often surprise, but at least it enables us to ascertain that even these skills are sometimes unequally distributed throughout the company and can, in certain cases, harm the effectiveness of the total range of services offered. One might also discover that it is better, in certain cases, quite simply to hive them off.

'Lever' skills call for close analysis. Are they always, in effect, levers? A few years ago, numerous large companies had their own printing shops, thus integrating a flexibility and quality which their local suppliers could not guarantee them. Others had their own hotel facilities, because what was available locally was too impersonal. Others again had gigantic data processing departments, because the software packages did not exist. What has become of all this paraphernalia today?

Are these skills of any value to the customer? Would it not be easier to 'buy' them on the market, as and when required?

Hiving off 'banal' and 'lever' skills can lead many companies along the road to becoming virtual, retaining only their key competences in their portfolio.

People and their knowledge

How do you know if you possess a skill essential to your company, or not? The diagram overleaf can enable you to set up your self-diagnosis. Skills and know-how are classified according to two criteria:

▨ the value which your knowledge represents for the customer;
▨ the ease with which you can be replaced in the exercise of this skill.

Your skill is only of interest if it represents a value for the customer. In addition, the company will be able to sell to the customer only if this value is unique – and thus difficult to replace.

Thomas Stewart, who designed this classification, proposes a framework for analysis using four fields.[3] You are located in the first

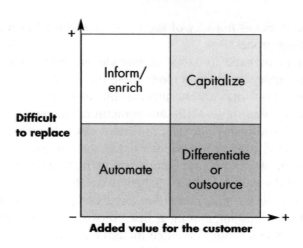

Source: after T. Stewart

two fields on the left *if your work presents a low added value for the customer*. This is in general the case with 'support functions'.

■ Your added value for the customer is low, it is easy to replace you (lower left field). Your situation is difficult, because your activity can be automated, even removed – those who punched subway tickets would undoubtedly have belonged to this category. In practice, the people who do this kind of work are most vulnerable. They are also those most easily transferred to other occupations if their qualifications are brought up to date or enriched. Today, electronic mail has revolutionized the way documents are transmitted; if your work consists in sorting and distributing mail, making photocopies, and so on, your future is compromised. To get out of this situation, you have to be made irreplaceable or your added value must be increased.

■ Your added value for the customer remains low but it is difficult to replace you (upper left field): you have technical skills necessary to the company, but not very useful for the customer. This is the case of the accounting department, of the various administrative posts, the 'support functions' necessary for the running of a company, but the profitability of which vis-à-vis the customer is not much in evidence. You may be lucky in that you may not be easily replaceable, but this cannot last. Increase your value by becoming an internal or external consultant. The day when your commercial value is brought into question you will be able to find customers elsewhere.

Juliette is responsible for the personnel resources of a medium-sized company, part-time. The rest of the time she does the same job on a time-sharing basis for several companies in the area. Everyone profits from this arrangement: her principal employer, who has the major benefit of her services at no great expense, as well as the experience Juliette accumulates working for her other customers. As for the latter, they benefit from the experience gained by Juliette in the larger company.

You have a significant added value for the customer. You are at the heart of a chain of added value within the company. In this case, there are two possible scenarios.

- You are easy to replace in spite of the service which you render to the customer. This is the case if you work in the fast-food catering business, newspaper distribution, or delivering pizzas. Admittedly, the service that you provide is important, but you can be replaced at the drop of a hat... unless your expertise increases so much that the customers demand to be served by you alone. If this is not the case, your company can decide to hive off your activity.

  This is more and more the situation of company delivery fleets. 'GT Location' and 'Féline', companies that specialized in hiring out vehicles with a driver, have their own training schools. Their drivers can do more than drive trucks; they can offer a complete service to the customer. The customer, looking for speed or caution, security or change, needs to be offered a flexible service. All customer-related professional services can further increase their added value: a cashier may meet with and advise customers, a bank clerk can sell insurance...

- Your customer added value is solid and irreplaceable. You are a star, someone that nobody can do without, neither the company, nor its customers. You possess strategic know-how; if you work in a service, you are undoubtedly already part of the management team. Otherwise, the company's competitors will be after you. You are at the heart of the intelligence capital of your company. The company will endeavour to capitalize on your knowledge by making it available to the other employees. You can refuse, but such reservation will make you vulnerable and reduce the degree of co-operation between the other employees of the company. In fact, to be fully applied, brilliant individual knowledge calls for the mobilization of the professional skills of many other people, replaceable or not, and of unequal added value, but of equal importance in the common effort to serve the customer.

Some, tempted by adventure, will leave, taking away their know-how and some methods borrowed from the company which had nurtured their success. Some succeed in reproducing and indeed going beyond the model they have left behind, others fail because certain essential skills remain behind in the previous company. These skills were not evident in the handbooks and the methods employed. They did not belong to any of the employees in particular. They still make up the strength of the company, and it is they that constitute its structural capital.

Each of us can thus analyse our know-how and work on our 'irreplaceability' and our added value. Of course, one can interpret this model with the four fields with cynicism. Some will see it as the basis of a policy for moving people on. The more realistic will discern in it a useful tool for self-analysis, enabling us to anticipate better, adapt better and change better.

In the same way, beyond the cynicism of a superficial reading, it is in the interest of a company to follow the same line of reasoning if it really wants to nurture the human capital at its disposal.

This is a game where the winner takes all, but no individual can walk away with the collective profits. This is the secret of learning.

The management of learning

In August 1997, Sodexho was awarded the contract for the logistics of a mass meeting of young people during the Pope's visit to France. The challenge was to feed 600,000 people for a week, one of the largest peacetime gatherings ever. To make a success of the operation was one challenge; to be able to reproduce it constituted the second. It was this second challenge that Laurent Cousin, the company's director of development, wanted to take up. On the one hand, it was a question of succeeding at something which had never been done before, and on the other of constantly monitoring oneself at work, in order to establish a *modus operandi* for managing similar gatherings in the future. Both operations were a success.

This kind of challenge has become common: it is no longer a question of simply reproducing carbon copies of the skills used every day; we have to be capable of inventing new skills at the heart of this daily activity. Learning has become commonplace. It is at the heart of the company, because the wealth to be created consists of information and knowledge.

The cycle of knowledge

Knowledge has its cycles, its economy. Initially it is part of the human cycle: knowledge only exists by virtue of the people who construct and bear it; it starts with perceived data, which becomes information, then knowledge. Knowledge is renewed so that intelligence can develop and adapt.

The cycle of learning runs through four distinct stages.

The first stage is *ignorance of the challenge* to come. I do not know what I do not know. This is the stage of refusal. Reality is being modified, but this information has not yet reached me. I have not yet perceived or felt anything. To get past this first stage we need signs, meetings, questions which will sow doubt in our minds and make us perceive new opportunities, new roads to travel. This is the time of dialogue, or rather the beginnings of it. When it is at the stage of skilful discussion, the company is only playing with its stock of knowledge without calling it into question, and without integrating anything new. When it is moving out of this stage, some scattered signs of renewal appear. The cycle of the knowledge is beginning.

The second stage is the *perception of change*, initially indistinct, then more and more specific; questions abound, but the fear of the unknown sometimes slows down the process of learning. I finally know that I do not know... I want to learn, and am afraid to learn. In order to move on to the following stage, we have to acknowledge and name the obstacles which arise so as better to overcome them; we have to transform the formless matter of knowledge into codified and identifiable knowledge. We have already referred to this stage of encoding when describing the languages of change. This is the painstaking work of decanting the images perceived by the right brain. Starting as images and formless ideas, they are gradually shaped into concepts through a process of abstraction. This stage of encoding is essential to make knowledge communicable. At this point, knowledge is in a state which we could call 'ready to wear'.

In the third stage, I know that I know. I have just acquired some knowledge and I am proud of it. I use it and think of it when I am using it. But to move on to the fourth stage, and in order that this knowledge may become collective knowledge, it has to be disseminated. The more such knowledge is found in an accessible and visible form, the easier it will be to transmit. After the innovative stage of concept construction, this is when the production process of the hypertext company begins. *The dissemination of knowledge* is at the heart of its trade. Knowledge will be the source of its productivity and inventiveness. This is the daily challenge facing the company, and it is a difficult one.

Many years ago, a particular global industrial company set up a team of 'skill watchers', who kept an inventory of the company's

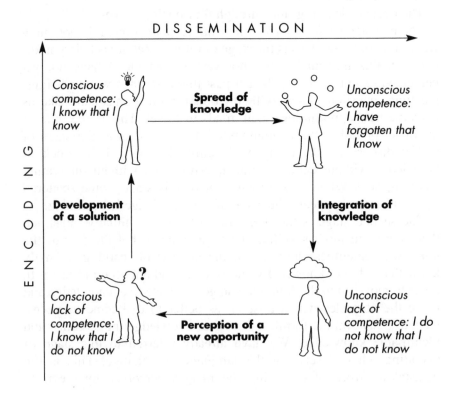

essential technologies and distinctive skills. At one point, however, the system ran out of steam. The 'watchers' felt isolated; they found it difficult to make themselves known, to identify new know-how and make it public. Then the Intranet arrived, and with it a simple idea: each person creates his or her 'homepage'. Now, using keywords and a simple search engine, it is possible to select those who are experts in a particular process, or the use of particular materials.

In the same way, the experience gained in a particular field, or a segment of the market, can be shared, on condition that it is stored in a simple database which can easily be accessed. This is what researchers and people at universities have been doing for a long time, exchanging questions and discoveries over the Internet.

If this process succeeds, we move on to the fourth stage. I have forgotten that I know: *knowledge has become a reflex*, and forms part of those tacit pools of knowledge which are now permanently embedded in the company and reinforce its structural capital. It is now a question of ensuring that this reflex becomes the prerogative of the whole company.

Apprenance (commitment to learning)

Annie talks to her customers, six hours a day, every day. One day one of them, intrigued, and amazed by her effectiveness and competence, asks: 'When do you take time to study, to learn all about these new products which your company introduces?' 'Every week', she replies, 'I "hide away" from my customers for five hours, which gives me time to reflect on their files, and to get to grips with the new products, the new services, the new techniques. We have arranged a special room for this purpose.'

Learning implies both teaching and the search for knowledge. The French neologism *apprenance* (translated here as 'commitment to learning') indicates a double movement. First, the individual will of people who want to develop their knowledge and skills, to improve their value to the customer in terms of their own irreplaceability, and second, the will of the company to find time, space and energy for the renewal of its knowledge capital.

'Commitment to learning', is the response to the company's need to develop its collective intelligence and to the need felt by each one of us to cultivate and increase our knowledge and skills.

Introducing 'commitment to learning', means giving learning the time, space and opportunity to nourish itself by dialogue, by action and by interaction. It means allowing the 'trees of knowledge' to grow.

The trees of knowledge[4]

The trees of knowledge, conceived originally for the educational world, are a model of the way in which knowledge circulates. They show that the 'commitment to learning' is not in fact just a double movement; when knowledge is mediated to others, the movement becomes triple. In fact, the to and fro of knowledge, by encoding and dissemination, ends up by becoming a collective good. Michel Authier and Pierre Lévy have produced a model of this triptych involving three 'universes' of knowledge.

The individual 'cognitive identity card', the first universe, is represented by a 'heraldic shield', the company is a 'tree', and the world of knowledge is represented by the 'patents'. The interaction between these three universes creates the hypertext company. People deposit their 'patents' in the bank of knowledge. Others, or perhaps the same people, acquire knowledge that has been 'patented' by learning.

The company 'tree' draws its nourishment from these knowledge 'patents', but retains a critical stance, choosing those which are useful and rejecting those which do not lead to growth. Conversely, it is people who, proud of their 'patents' and of what they have learned, trim and shape the company tree. In return, the 'heraldic shield', which is a recognition of the knowledge and skills they have placed at the service of the company, gathers under its banner the individual skills offered to customers, and creates a 'company fellowship', working together to offer a service in common.

Leif Edvinsson, of Skandia, has also constructed a similar model, called 'The Navigator', which allows for the guidance of the acquisition and dissemination of intellectual capital. Other such models will no doubt be invented. Intellectual capital has become a strategic tool. On the other hand, whatever the quality of the model used, knowledge will not be produced, stored and developed unless people want to learn and to exchange their knowledge.

The robin, the titmouse and the bottle of milk

How does learning take place? Arie de Geus, former director of development at Shell, was one of the very first to work on this subject. He is the author of the famous quotation: 'To be competitive is to learn more quickly than the others.' In his search for learning techniques, he encountered Allan Wilson, a zoologist at Berkeley.[5] Listening to him he discovered that although man may be the most advanced species in the world in terms of learning, birds constitute the second most advanced species. One thing in particular distinguishes them: because of their relative 'youth' in terms of the history of living species, their speed of learning is remarkable. It does not take place from generation to generation, as in the case of most other species, but within the generations themselves. In support of his thesis, he told a true story, which in France would seem like one of La Fontaine's fables. Here is the fable of the robin, the titmouse and the bottle of milk.

The story took place in England, where fresh milk bottles are placed each morning on the doorsteps outside the houses. For a long time they were not fitted with tops, and domestic birds, titmice and robins, got into the habit of feeding on the cream on top. Between the two wars, the milk distributors decided to protect the milk by capping the bottles with aluminium tops. Some robins managed to pierce the tops, but the majority of them had to find another source of food. At the beginning of the 1950s, in contrast to the robins, the whole titmouse population knew how to drill through the aluminium caps and once more had access to this rich source of food. What had happened?

Allan Wilson offered three avenues of explanation. It all began with innovation, shared by robins and titmice alike, who both found new ways of reaching the milk. Some individuals, titmice or robins, succeeded in drilling through the aluminium tops. But a few individuals do not make a population. A second condition came into operation: 'how should this innovative knowledge be spread?' In this respect, titmice and robins would seem to be equal: the same quality of song, the same richness of colours and movement, but, said Wilson, there was a third reason that made the difference. In spring, the titmice raise their young, but at the beginning of the summer they leave their nests and move from garden to garden in small bands of eight or ten. This period lasts two or three months. The robins, in contrast, remain in their territory, using their song to drive away intruders. Mobility, then, was the third reason that made all the difference. Learning takes place through the propagation of knowledge, and in order to propagate it we have to travel and mix people together. Transposed to the situation facing a company, this story is very revealing. Companies of 'robins', where each specialist defends his territory and jealously protects his knowledge, are more common than 'titmouse' companies, where individuals learn in groups, with no concern for age, rank, speciality or territory. Are you a titmouse or a robin?

Team learning

The way the titmice learned is an example of team learning. Educational experts know the value of co-operative learning,[6] learning in common, where each person is both teacher and pupil, but team learning is still not a very widespread practice. Here are four very simple rules for making progress along these lines.[7]

The first rule is obvious: *the team has to set itself an objective.* If the objective is launched from above, there will be no effect. You can only answer a question you yourself have posed in the first place. If this is not the case, the exercise becomes academic and ends up losing its direction. It is not easy to set an objective. Very often, those who in terms of their profession have stopped learning are convinced that they have reached the limits of their development. They have reached the top, and this is at the same time their pride and their secret fear. All future development is blocked if there is no longer anything to assimilate or learn.

The second rule *means entrusting the search for answers to those who raised the question.* Brigitte and Janine are sales assistants. In the course of their teamwork, they had decided to tackle certain problems relating to the credit account. Errors connected with prices, quantity and product confusion had been increasing during the previous months. If they had followed the traditional procedure, the sales manager would have said to them: 'Very well, we will ask the accounts department to make a thorough analysis of the causes of these credit problems and suggest some solutions to us.' This step, apparently effective enough, would in fact have killed off the 'commitment to learning'. The solution which was therefore proposed was to entrust the file to Brigitte and Janine. They went to consult the 'experts' in the accounts department, charted the causes of the credit problems, then, at the next meeting, and in the presence of the financial people, made suggestions for improvements.

The third rule, directly inspired by the activities of the titmice, *consists in inviting to each meeting someone from another department*, whose task will be to play 'dumb', and ask some common-sense questions. Moreover, the presence of people from other departments allows us to attack our working methods from all sides at the outset.

The fourth and last rule is *to invite our customers to join us in the search for answers*. This is not always easy. Often, though, because we are afraid or unaccustomed to the idea, we do not dare invite them in, forgetting that customers will more often than not be flattered than offended by such an invitation.

Team learning does not stop with these few rules. Those involved have to co-operate, to emulate each other. Each of us must acquire this talent of joint learning, which consists of dialogue, trust, a sincere desire to find the truth, and humility in the face of the knowledge of others. Those teams which have known for a long time how to develop these talents are often those that innovate: research teams, advertising agencies, sales teams... in each case, behind all the inventiveness, one can discern an astonishing network of confidence and respect in which people have known how to share sufferings as well as victories.

Team learning is not easy. When this point has been reached, however, how is this taste for learning to be transmitted to the rest of the company?

The learning company – a map

The four stages of learning presented above each correspond to the same number of activities that have to be organized throughout the whole company.

The first group, the watchers, should prepare the company for the raising of questions in the future that can call its whole line of business into question. Those who keep vigil should be totally immersed in the company's activities, and yet open to the winds of change. This could be the scientific committee of a large company, or the network of researchers who gravitate around small, innovative companies.

A second group will then make public the information or knowledge which the company must acquire to renew its skills. There will often be the temptation to entrust to the members of the first group the task of encoding and publishing the information collected. This will often be a mistake. Keeping watch and making information public are two different 'trades'. Watchers are voyagers; the others are scribes.

The third group are the storytellers. They will pass on this knowledge, this information within the company. Traditionally, these will be the training units who design the training programmes for the various groups of professional skills within the company. Today, their role is often difficult when the content to be transmitted has not been nurtured and renewed by the first two groups. The knowledge that they transmit is nicely organized, but obsolete.

One can also imagine a fourth and broader group, which would be connected to the first three to ensure that they (the latter) were working in the same direction as the rest of the company. This is what I have called the 'arts and crafts' group; the 'arts' of the right brain and

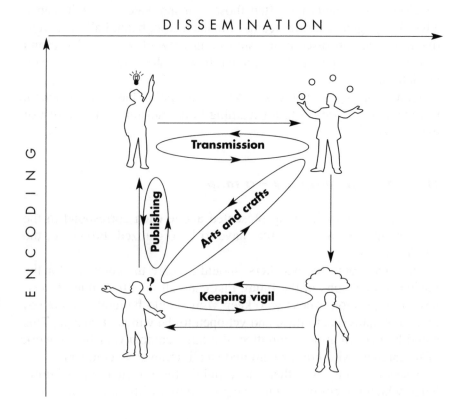

the 'crafts' of the left brain working together to enrich action. This group could take various forms, depending on the company. It could be a brotherhood, or an annual gathering, or an innovation forum such as that used by Sodexho and Air Liquide to present their best practices. It could also be the educational display boards used by the Volvo workers in Ghent to publicize the solutions that have been found to various problems. It could even simply be the induction meetings arranged by a company for new employees, or general training courses covering all aspects of the company: 'Everything you have ever wanted to know about our company and have never dared to ask!' These four groups, or four interlocking loops, exist, more or less, in the majority of companies, but those leaders who have made them their personal and regular business are far too rare. Rarer still are those who have placed these four groups in the centre of the daily activities of their company in order to make it a real learning company.

The rules of learning or of 'commitment to learning' can more or less be described, like those relating to dialogue or 'knowing how to become'. One thing is certain, however: companies that apply them at once will take a decisive lead. This lead they will owe in part to the quasi-natural use of these tools of action, dialogue and learning, but also to those leaders who did not hesitate to leave traditional forms of organization behind, ready to discover and assume new responsibilities.

Notes

1. Lao-Tseu, *La Voie et sa vertu: Tao-tê-king*, Points Seuil, 1979.
2. Quoted by Edgar Morin, CJD Congress at Lille, June 1990.
3. Thomas A. Stewart, *Intellectual Capital*, New York, Currency Doubleday, 1997.
4. Michel Authier and Pierre Lévy, *Les Arbres de connaissances*, Paris, La Découverte, 1996.
5. Arie de Geus, *The Living Company*, Boston, MA, Harvard Business Press, 1997.
6. Robert Pléty, *L'Apprentissage co-opérant*, Lyon, Presses Universitaires de Lyon, 1996.
7. Manfred Mack and the present author headed a commission set up by the CNPF in 1996 to look at the learning company.

10 The Lessons of Hernán Cortés

ENTERPRISE

> A voyage of one mile and a voyage of a thousand both begin with the first step.
>
> Lao-Tseu

Does the hypertext company need a leader? Undoubtedly, but the role has changed. In terms of the actual work of the company, the leader has become less and less useful, and his traditional tasks – planning, organizing, implementing, controlling – have now been delegated to those who work closest to the customer. The traditional leader always held the floor and had the last word, but the hypertext company has more need of dialogue to build up a common vision. In the same way, the monopoly of knowledge often held by the traditional leader has fallen into disuse; the hypertext company today can renew its skills through the permanent learning process. The hypertext company needs a leader who can guarantee the spirit of enterprise, a balanced programme of action, and the proper husbanding of the energy sources that power the whole process.

Movement

A warm breeze bearing the scent of bougainvillaea wafted across the gardens and nonchalantly stirred the palms which rustled against the blue rectangle of the window. It was difficult to concentrate on the project which was the reason for our gathering. In an attempt to get the economy moving, the Mexican government had decided to instigate the creation of one new company per day in each province of the country over the following two or three years. To serve this project, the team to which I as a young graduate had the singular honour of belonging was to conceive, organize and set up for the country as a whole an information processing system which would make it possible to locate, evaluate, select and finance the projects.

This seminar took place at Cuernavaca, in an old hacienda which had belonged to Hernán Cortés, the famous conquistador. His adventure was the antithesis of our rational, technocrat approach. He had left Spain to discover the mythical Eldorado, and built the whole of his conquest of Mexico on intuition, bluff and chance, on the quasi-impromptu use of natural forces and men.

However, this project did not create any commercial ventures, as there were no entrepreneurs. To create a commercial enterprise you have to invent a goal, to clear a way to reach it, and share both of these things with those working alongside you. There, precisely, are the three lessons to be learned from Cortés.

First lesson: inventing the goal

On 18 February 1519, Hernán Cortés left Cuba to conquer Mexico before Diego Velasquez, the Spanish governor who had entrusted to him a simple reconnaissance mission on the coasts of Yucatan, was able to relieve him of his command. While Velasquez sought – and found – other minor decisions to take, Cortés 'invented' his own goal: the conquest of Mexico and all its riches. His whole fortune was invested in the 11 ships which weighed anchor that day, carrying with them 100 sailors, 500 soldiers, 14 guns and 16 horses.

Enterprise is what starts the whole ball rolling; there is no industrial enterprise without an entrepreneur. More than ever, the essential role of the leader is to invent the goal. Today, the hypertext company releases him from all those daily decisions which he formerly ended up drowning in, deciding everything and nothing, borne along by the current of events and weighed down with the 'monkeys' randomly thrust upon him at meetings and chance encounters. Information circulates so quickly now that he can longer put off decisions on the pretext that he is awaiting the vessel bringing orders from the King of Spain.

Finding the goal means defining, redefining and constantly calling into question the product range offered by the company. Emmanuel d'André, President of Trois Suisses International, has summarized his company's position as follows: 'We have changed a lot in order not to change our trade, which is distance selling.' Finding the goal means guessing at and then identifying major market trends, outlining new ambitions, pushing back the frontiers, unlearning the old styles and suggesting new rules for the game. It means choosing a strategy, the essential mediator between the dream and the will to act, between what is desirable and what is possible, between the resources to be kept in reserve and those which have to be mobilized. 'One has to be a visionary, an entrepreneur and an investor at one and the same time',[1] if one is to unite all the partners of the company in the service of the aim: shareholders, suppliers, customers and employees. The goal has really got to be worth the trouble!

Second lesson: intuition shows the way

Malinche, a young Indian captive, revealed to Cortés the weaknesses and the fears of the Aztecs; thanks to her, he was able to exploit the famous prediction of the avenging return of the god, Quetzalcóalt, turning this reincarnation to his own advantage.

Being enterprising means choosing a different road to go down. How many companies have not owed their success to their 'positioning', as much as, if not more than, to their product? From the creation of the global market place to the arrival of the Internet, the roads leading to the new 'market space' are many and varied. How many companies, though, through lack of imagination or courage (sometimes both), continue to reproduce the well-trodden paths of their organizations?

Just as the *vision of the goal* is not taught in any school of management, the *intuition of the way* requires a certain independence of mind. One needs to be a nomad, divergent, iconoclastic, shaping one's decisions on the move. Among the plethora of ordinary events, one has to be able to discern and distinguish those that bear the signs of a new road to travel. These are all instances of intuition. The intuition of the way is a mere glance transformed into action. Knowing how to look means knowing how to use time, a priceless strategic reserve. Those who are prisoners of time, with their backs to the wall and forever harried by urgency, do not decide, but only react. Breaking out of the prison of time means setting aside time for the journey and time for dialogue, two instances of 'time' which are often only one. The way to follow is paved with intense presence and attentive absence, with moments of rare decision and by delegation at every instant – by a mind, a diary and an office empty of routines and open to new projects!

Third lesson: the uncertainty of risks shared

Montezuma, the superstitious emperor, informed hour by hour of the advance of the Spaniards, hesitates still, doubtful of what decision to take: who is Cortés? A god, invincible and avenging, or only a simple man, covetous and vulnerable? Cortés, for his part, exploited this uncertainty which in the end would kill Montezuma.

Uncertainty, like information, nourishes decisions; our hyper-informed world has not killed it off. So much the better: it is a guarantee and a promise of freedom, opportunity, inventiveness. Leadership means giving uncertainty perspective and direction, mobilizing it to provide a lever to move the future. Sharing this uncertainty means revealing that quantum leap which will have to be taken. It means exposing at the same time both the difficulty of the task and the accessibility (because it is shared) of the goal.

The entrepreneur has no problems motivating people: the vision of the goal and the choice of the road to take are enough to make people want to work with him. If managers experience motivation problems among their employees, it is because they have not set up a goal and shown a way towards it in which the employees can mirror their own goals and chosen ways. We are motivated both by the goal and by the way towards it. The task of sharing the uncertainty of success cannot be delegated; uncertainty, like the devil, feeds on details. It is therefore necessary to keep your eyes on the horizon and watch where you are putting your feet, at each step!

Uncertainty should not be allowed to kill initiative and the spirit of decision. In order to get a company moving, you have to decide; and deciding calls for a strong wish to discover the future. In a traditional company, the art of decision-making was reserved for the chosen few, whereas in a hypertext company it is exercised by the largest possible number. To decide has always been an activity involving both reason and intuition. It means moving more and more away from reproductive decision-making to creative decision-making, from rational thought to the intuitive glance put into action, from disquieting infor-

mation to serene uncertainty. Once the decision has been taken, the
company is on the move. At this point, the question of balance arises.

Balance

Movement calls for a balance between body and mind, between
reason and feelings. This is the balance between action, dialogue and
learning. If one of these dimensions is in imbalance, the company
loses its equilibrium. In this context, the leader is the master and guarantor of balance, a tightrope walker and rope-dancer, both architect
and gardener.

Rope-dancer and architect

The first point of balance is *in action itself*; the action of the company
is no longer sequential, but simultaneous, in a constant process of
being formed. This permanent metamorphosis is not possible unless
the vision of the goal is always present. The role of the leader is to
build and share this vision, which will make it possible both to create
the future and to act in the present. Each person must hold the keys of
day-to-day action in order to be able to act and to make changes
without unpleasant surprises, keeping as close as possible to the
customer who is to be served.

Balance is also found in the authority behind the action. The
authority of a leader is essentially expressed in his ability to transform
his employees into 'authors': authors of their own action, their own
dialogue, their own learning. This authority is not a question of
decree, nor can it be taught. It is learned. Thereafter, it is measured in
terms of the results produced by the company. It is easy enough to
evaluate the profitability of financial capital; the necessary formulas
abound, whether your company is noted on the Stock Exchange or
not. On the other hand, measurement of the effective use of the intellectual capital has yet to be developed. There are many factors to be
considered: the development of patents, the time spent with
customers, the maintenance of databases, the part played by new
products or services in the financial returns, the time spent on training
per employee, added value per capita, the quality of the processes that

lead to dialogue, and so on. Certain ways of measuring these factors already exist, others will have to be invented.

The second point of balance is found *in dialogue*. The responsibility of the leader is very clear here. He has to provide the time and space for dialogue and an atmosphere in which it can take place. Dialogue time is not the time spent on meetings which revolve round skilful and polished discussions. If we want time for dialogue we have to ensure that people have the right to speak and the right to remain silent. Managing this 'dialogue space' means organizing impromptu meetings: connecting those who would pass by without seeing each other if the doors were not open, the chairs drawn up and coffee ready. To establish dialogue we have to sacrifice the traditional rituals connected with calling meetings. Even so, it is impossible to guarantee the production of dialogue: as we have seen, dialogue cannot be established by decree. At the same time, preventing people expressing their opinions or asking questions will not establish the co-operation desired. 'In order to innovate', declares Pierre Bellon, President of Sodexho, 'a company must know how to protect the innovator from the hierarchy.'

The third point of balance is found *in learning*. The first responsibility of the leader is to guarantee that learning is moving in the right direction, which is also that of the company, related to its present and future utility. To develop useless skills is a waste of time; but at the same time, skills without customers are equally useless. Even the most brilliant degree does not create a pool of goodwill on its own. Learning develops when knowledge is directed to action and the service of the customer. Conversely, not to develop skills needed by the company and its customers is unforgivable negligence. This is the second responsibility of the leader, and rests on a whole complex of skills: 'researcher, midwife, gardener and architect', wrote Bob Aubrey[2] and Alain Gauthier, pioneers of the 'learning company' concept.

The *researcher* acknowledges that it is in the process of research that he 'does not know'. This is also the first stage of learning. He admits his ignorance with humility but displays with pleasure his curiosity and obstinacy. It is his task to share these things with others, leaving the door open for the dialogue, the emergence of the doubt, new intuitions and disturbing ideas, confident in the ability of his employees to come up with an answer.

He is also a *midwife*. This is the second stage. This process of supporting by speech and gesture the birth of an idea, a strategy, a process or a product calls for much patience and for an attentive, solicitous presence. It is tempting to draw back and let the others deal with the problem, but it is equally dangerous to do the work for them. The learning capacity of the company lies somewhere between 'monkeys' and 'Teflon'. It is also dangerous to leave the discoverers alone with their discovery, no matter how imposing it is. Christopher Columbus, the discoverer of the New World, was not a trained manager. The new idea has to be viable, and encoded so that it can be understood and accepted by all, and for this reason it has to be exposed to the criticism of other members of the company, and of its partners. Training teams far removed from the presence of customers end up going round in circles.

He is an *architect*. This is the third stage, that of dissemination. The new piece of knowledge, the new idea, must irrigate and fertilize the company. The architect builds up the structural capital, from the daily work to the process of innovation, using all those routines of knowledge which are the strength of companies that can learn, invent and apply knowledge to action. He will also have to pull down certain older 'houses of knowledge', which originally accommodated and supported the intelligence of the company, but in the end have become its prison. He will also need to learn how to preserve, restructure and resuscitate other bodies of knowledge, which when brought together in a new way will strengthen the whole company.

Finally, he is a *gardener*. This is the fourth stage. Knowledge has become a wealth owned by all. The gardener has become a master of the art of cultivating these ordinary, but essential plants: ignorance and curiosity, dialogue and silence, divergent and convergent thinking. These are the qualities on which the company feeds, but which only belong to the people who possess them.

Charting the company

To ensure the balance between action, dialogue and learning, we have to draw up a map of the company showing these various fields of balance. The diagram overleaf, drawn from the example of a real company, may open up some avenues of approach. It is a question of locating, within each of these three essential axes of balance, the places, the moments, the structures and the actors that will contribute to the creation and maintenance of this fragile and necessary balance between action, dialogue and learning.

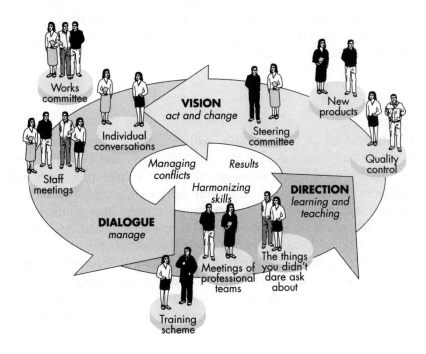

Dialogue

So, what place will you reserve for dialogue? Works committees, union representatives, staff representatives: the juridical forms of social dialogue are of course necessary, but they are seldom sufficient. When formalism carries the day, dialogue is replaced by debates and skilful discussions. The opinions expressed only represent certainties, and leave little room for that reciprocal questioning and exploration essential to the establishment of dialogue. Dialogue needs space, time, signs: it is necessary to know how to alternate the size of the groups and the degree of formality of meetings, always keeping in mind that whatever the group produces must be visible if dialogue is to become an accepted practice in the company. It has to be shown that dialogue produces ideas, new attitudes and new ways of seeing and understanding reality. Company newsletters and other tools of communication are used to attract new proselytes of dialogue, active listening and other values; why, then, is their effect so restricted? Jean Cocteau once wrote: 'There is no love, only the proofs of love.' Charting the company in terms of dialogue will also reveal how much space and time is appropriated by one-track meetings which prevent dialogue, stifle action and impoverish learning.

Action

The place of action is often more visible, but less attention is paid to the places and moments which control, diversify and evaluate it. We are familiar with board meetings and their formal rites, and with steering committees which deal with daily events and with change. There are also the more modest meetings of teams that do their business in the blink of an eye, or which spend hours tracing back a network of possible causes in order better to understand a breakdown, to accelerate a particular process or to serve a customer. Digital photographs, e-mail and video conferences are new interactive factors which can be added to the list of essential briefings and debriefings – too often neglected – which are the secret of powerful companies.

Learning

How much space and time will you devote to learning? The speed and urgency of life have made us forget that we need time for learning. It is the task of the leader to establish the basic rhythms of work in the company, but it is also part of the leader's job to create the necessary spaces, structures and channels for dialogue, innovation and learning. Using the map of learning presented above, one can identify the points at which the leader should intervene. In the first place, he must ensure that these four learning groups ('learning loops') are kept moving, regenerate themselves and are productive in the service of the company. The professional teams that are an integral part of the fourth cycle are living proof that the permanent presence of the customer provides direction and strength. As soon as the customer is absent from its thinking, the learning cycle weakens and the team begins to run round in circles. The leader must also make sure that there are strong links between the various learning groups. The new technology waiting on the threshold will certainly be able to provide the company with the information that is most relevant, and rich in terms of innovation, but it is likely to be ineffective if conformism, routine and the fear of innovation keep it waiting outside. In this case, a leader has to be 'insolent' in what is etymologically the root sense of the word: bringing to the company what it is not in the habit of hearing or seeing. The same applies to the second group, the editors: the work schedule and the plans that have been formed have been brought within range of the company, but are very likely to call its whole organization into question, and at this point the fear of cutting into the bone, of introducing a revolution into the company, will perhaps hold it back.

How many companies, now defunct, had invented, developed, even perfected a new product or a new service which they never put on the market out of fear of losing their image, their privileges or their comfortable existence, while their erstwhile competitors, now leaders in the field, wasted no time on useless heart-searching or introspection and took the risk of inventing something new and of reinventing themselves at the same time? The third group requires even more refined management. It draws together all training systems within the company, and is firmly established; but can one be sure that it is passing on the skills of tomorrow, rather than those of yesterday? Is it making the company convergent or divergent? The competence of a company is measured in terms of quality rather than the possession of a well-ordered body of knowledge.

Breaking out of conformism, not being afraid to take major steps, establishing common codes: these are all essential tasks facing the leader in this new, but increasingly central field of learning – almost the only real tool that can renew the intellectual capital of a company.

Eco-nomy

The third responsibility of the leader is the management of energy sources. The intricate workings of a hypertext company are not virtual: harmony of movement and the force that maintains equilibrium rest on these essential sources of energy that power and maintain the activities of the company.

One tends immediately to think of financial capital, that of shareholders or creditors. In this connection, recently developed concepts, such as that of EVA (economic value added) or MVA (market value added), provide leaders with a whole palette of methods to apply.

These methods are widely known and widely used today, and we shall not return to them here.

On the other hand, the economy of intellectual capital has yet to be constructed. The word 'economy' may seem surprising in this context, but it is taken here in its literal meaning. Like the words 'ecology' or 'ecosystem', the word 'economy' is made up of the Greek root *oikia*, which indicates 'home' or 'family' – in short, our common heritage – and the ending '-nomy'. This ending indicates classification, hierarchy, management: in the present case, the management of the company's intellectual heritage. The intellectual capital is a type of capital which has to be managed and augmented.

Management

We have just devoted the three preceding chapters to an outline of the management of intellectual capital in the context of a hypertext company. The diagram shown here summarizes the essential points. The components of intellectual capital bear fruit in action, dialogue and learning, which are manifestations of human activity on the part of both customer and producer.

In terms of action, managing intellectual capital means first and foremost utilizing customer capital as well as possible, moving from blind transaction to partnership. This is not possible unless the people involved are able at the same time to develop that initiative and autonomy which are essential if the information system which little by

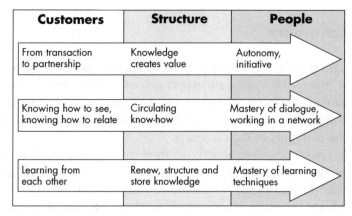

little will enrich the relationship to the customer is to be fully opera-
tive. This action is enriched by the dialogue which company
employees are able to establish, both among themselves and with the
customer. Thus, in a relatively simple manner, that process of reciprocal learning is set up, the process which constructs, passes on and
turns into company capital those fields of knowledge which the
company places at the disposal of its customers.

Return

There are innumerable ways of remunerating financial capital. Each
day, new formulas, simple or sophisticated, swell the financial
columns of the media. On the other hand, people are more hesitant
regarding the remuneration of intellectual capital.

Customer capital is remunerated directly, following the bias of the
market: the customer decides to place or not to place his 'capital' of
confidence and trust in your hands. In order to preserve this capital
and make it multiply, one has in the first place to be keenly aware of
its reality, its importance – and its fickleness. These tasks are the
prime responsibility of the leaders, the guardians of the company
heritage. Ensuring the loyalty of this customer capital means anticipating the dreams of the consumer, the supplier, of all those to whom
the company can and wishes to be useful. It means putting oneself in
their place in order better to understand them. Finally, it means
making them 'work', using their imagination to build with them a
competitive added value which can be placed at their service. The
company must then capitalize on this added value, destined to become
a 'pearl of great price' which will increase and multiply in the future.

Human capital is different. It does not belong to the company, but
the bond that attaches it to the company is more basic and more
durable, expressing perhaps an even greater degree of dependency.
Augmenting human capital means remunerating people in various
ways: apart from wages, they can be given a share in the company's
profits, a practice which is recognized but not widespread. Increasingly, too, it is a question of helping them to develop their added value
to the customer and their 'irreplaceability'. Cynics will retort that a
company can have no interest in developing the irreplaceability of its
employees, and this may be true if it is simply regarded as expenditure. It is not true if the employees add their skills to the company's

pool, or capital, of intelligence. To quote a saying of Hervé Sérieyx: 'Enterprise is not a solitary act, but one of solidarity.' The IQ of the company is more than the product of the individual IQs.

Structural capital, for its part, is residual. Situated at the place where the customers and all the other human actors meet, it belongs to the company and the company must make it bear fruit, but we must be careful not to forget the fundamental law which indissolubly links the three types of intelligence capital: even the best data banks need the human touch of the people who bring them to life, and the interest of the customers who make of them something useful.

Notes

1. Jacques Barraux, 'L'Amérique réinvente nos entreprises', *l'Expansion*, No. 535, November 1996.
2. *Savoir faire savoir,* op. cit.

Conclusion

Globalization, networks and information have changed the nature of work and transformed society. The traditional company is on its deathbed; it will be succeeded by hypertext companies. Lighter and more complex, such companies are stronger but more ephemeral. The role played by people is wider than before, but more demanding. They contribute their intelligence to the company, but do they get their just returns? Did they ever? Human capital and customer capital do not belong to this new type of company, which concentrates on developing its structural capital: less visible, but often more productive than the financial capital.

The hypertext company is only in its infancy. We have been so occupied in making the quantum leap between two worlds that we have not yet written the statutes on which it is based. We have only listed its energy sources, as well as the principles and the few rules which will help it to grow.

The purpose of this book has been to show that these new principles which have altered the nature of work and changed society, have also radically transformed the resources and the organization of companies: companies move and breathe in a different world.

In this sense they are more than ever created in our image: they can be impassioned and capricious, generous and forgetful, interdependent and yet egoistic. Companies are made up of 'the others', co-operating with 'the others', and yet they are more than ever 'themselves'. In the time to come, contracts, rules and the laws will be married little by little with the profile of these new companies, with the desires and the duties of these people and those people.

It is still early to detail these changes, but it is too late to turn back.

We have moved on to a new century. For some, the quantum leap is still to come, while others have already begun the next dance. The music, hesitant at first, is slowly building up, but the rhythm is already there: complex, rich, and much, much faster than before.

Bibliography

Albert, Eric. *Comment devenir un bon stressé*. Paris, Odile Jacob, 1994

Aubrey, Bob. *Le Travail après la crise*. Paris, InterEditions, 1994

Authier, Michel and Lévy, Pierre. *Les Arbres de connaissances*. Paris, La Découverte, 1996

Barber, Benjamin R. *Djihad versus McWorld*. Paris, Desclée de Brouwer, 1996

Jean Boissonnat Commission. *Le travail dans vingt ans*. Paris, Odile Jacob, 1996

Bruhnes, Bernard Consultants (Directed by Danielle Kaisergruber). *Négocier la flexibilité*. Paris, Les Editions d'Organization, 1997

Carfantan, Jean-Yves. *L'Epreuve de la mondialisation*. Paris, Seuil, 1996

Chaize, Jacques. *La Porte du changement s'ouvre de l'intérieur*. Paris, Calmann-Lévy, 1992

Centre des Jeunes Dirigeants d'Entreprise (CJD). *L'Entreprise au XXIème siècle*. Paris, Flammarion, 1996

Cohen, Daniel. *Richesses du monde, pauvretés des nations*. Paris, Flammarion, 1997

Damasio, Antonio R. *Descartes' Error. Emotion, Reason and the Human Brain*. Grosset/Putman, 1994

De Geus, Arie. *The Living Company*. New York, Harvard Press, 1997

Demuth, Gérard. *Rien n'est pareil, mais çà n'est pas un drame*. Paris, Stock, 1997

D'Iribarne, Philippe. *Vous serez tous des maîtres*. Paris, Seuil, 1996

Edvinsson, Leif (in collaboration with Michael Malone). *Intellectual Capital*. New York, Harper Business, 1997

Fukuyama, Francis. *Trust*. New York, Free Press, 1995

Grove, Andrew. *Only the Paranoid Survive*. New York, Currency Doubleday, 1996

Lasfargue, Yves. *Robotisés, rebelles, rejetés*. Paris, Editions de l'Atelier, 1993

Hamel, Gary and Prahalad, C.K. *Competing for the Future*. Boston, MA, Harvard Business School Press, 1994

Mack, Manfred. *Co-évolution, dynamique créatrice*. Paris, Village Mondial, 1997

Méda, Dominique. *Le Travail, une valeur en voie de disparition*. Paris, Aubier, 1995

Mermet, Gérard. *Francoscopie*. Paris, Larousse, 1997

Moore, James F. *The Death of Competition*. New York, John Wiley & Sons, 1996

Patrenôtre, Raymond. *Voulons-nous sortir de la crise?* Paris, Plon, 1934
Pléty, Robert. *L'Apprentissage co-opérant.* Lyon, Presses Universitaires de Lyon, 1996
Senge, Peter. *Fifth Discipline Field Book.* New York, Doubleday, 1994
Stewart, Thomas A. *Intellectual Capital.* New York, Currency Doubleday, 1997
Thureau-Mangin, Philippe. *La Concurrence et la mort.* Paris, Syros, 1995
Thurow, Lester. *The Future of Capitalism.* London, NB Publishing, 1996
Watzlawick, Paul. *Munchhausen's Pigtail, or Psychotherapy and 'Reality' Essays and Lectures.* New York, W.W. Norton, May 1990
Watzlawick, Paul. *The Language of Change: Elements of Therapeutic Communication.* New York, W.W. Norton, 1993

Index